# BIRTH MOTHER

*Memoir of a Woman who Chose Adoption for her Infant*

*Author's 1965 high school graduation photo*

*By Judith Ellen Bock*

# Table of Contents

# Dedication

To the grandchildren I will likely never meet but who might want to know something of their mother's origins. To women and girls faced with unplanned pregnancies who seek information to make an informed decision. Most of all, to my daughter who bravely agreed to meet me, if only for the first and only time since her birth.

# Acknowledgements

I am grateful to my husband Glenn, niece Kathy, friend Cindy and numerous others who have supported me in my search to find my daughter and to write this memoir. To my draft readers who suggested many needed changes and offered support to complete and publish this book: Kathy S., Kathy T., Cindy and Carla. A special thanks to Nancy and Mary Helen, my local adoption triad support group's dedicated co-founder and searcher respectively. Together, we tried to help many people separated by the secrecy of closed adoptions.

# About the Author

At the age of 22 Judith Bock placed her infant daughter into an adoptive home and attempted to get on with her life believing she had "done the right thing." Years later she began to deal with the unresolved grief of giving her baby to strangers.

In her memoir, Bock tells of her journey to resolve this grief, detailing early life influences, the pregnancy, birth and adoption, failed marriages, activities in adoption triad groups, and counseling. She ultimately searches for, finds and meets her lost daughter.

Bock graduated from St. John's School of Nursing in Springfield, Missouri, in 1968. She worked as a registered nurse in Missouri, Oklahoma, Illinois, and Wisconsin.

She graduated magna cum laude with a Bachelor of Journalism from the University of Missouri in 1997 and worked in public relations and free-lance writing. She combined her medical and journalism knowledge as a health coach before retiring in 2012.

She lives in central Missouri with her husband Glenn, cat Rosie and dog Lily.

# Preface

April 1, 2019

I have started this book in fictionalized versions several times before. I've never been able to finish it to my satisfaction. This attempt may turn out the same. I tried at one point to get an agent for the fictional version, and one expressed interest but rejected it. I don't know all the reasons why I have been unsuccessful in telling my story previously. Perhaps I am reluctant to take another chance at a book rejection. No doubt, I wish to avoid revisiting a painful subject.

It could be simple laziness. Or the desire to move forward and stop looking back. Getting busy with other things is another factor. But here I go again, this time with a new plan and resolve.

I will try the "Bird-by Bird" approach of completing a complex and overwhelming task as described by a favorite spiritual author, Ann Lamotte. The idea is not to complete a complicated project in a short period, let alone one sitting, but to do it a bit at a time, bird by bird, as her brother did with the last-minute homework assignment about birds. Maybe a couple of pages on Mondays, Wednesdays, and Fridays, a chapter a month, or what I find most appealing, 35 minutes in one sitting.

We'll see how it goes. I promise my readers that this will be a work of honesty. I may leave some sensitive personal information out, but what I do write will be the truth as I know and remember. I will change some names and locations to maintain the privacy of some people I write about. I will try not to be judgmental about others depicted, but I probably won't be entirely successful with this.

I have tried to forgive myself for giving away my flesh and blood child, and I have made some progress with this. I doubt this will ever be complete.

Why am I writing this, you might ask? I will be 72 years old, about a week from today, on April 8, 2019. My daughter will turn 50 the day before. This book is not for her. I don't believe she will read it. She's not too interested in me it seems. She doesn't want us to get to know each other, at least for now. We can get into that later.

This may be for her children, my grandchildren by blood, who I don't know. Maybe they will be curious. It is also for others who are curious and want to learn how a woman could give away a baby. After all, in the days we now live in, many young, single women get pregnant, sometimes intentionally, sometimes not, but would not consider giving away their own child.

This is for me because a voice inside keeps telling me I need to do this. I am unsure where it comes from, but I want to silence that voice. Is it the creative force most people refer to as God or the Divine Presence, the latter as named by spiritual writer Macrina Wiederkehr? Another name for God that Wiederkehr uses is O Divine Wrestler, which may be appropriate for this writing odyssey. Oh, Divine Presence, you must keep prodding me with that voice if you want me to complete this memoir. You may have to wrestle me away from the retirement activities I prefer.

Despite the fear of redundancy, I want to add my story to the many that have already been written concerning this topic. But of course, it will be unique. I am the only me, and my daughter is her only self. Only I have the source material. That source is my memory and several files, a notebook, and photos. These I've collected over the years and add to my "awakening" to the profound event of transferring the parentage of my child to others.

v

For privacy purposes, I have changed some names, including my daughter's. Neither the names "Jody" nor "Rose" is her legal name.

My cat Rosie is on my lap now, watching my fingers peck away at my reasonably old laptop. I suspect she will be a frequent companion for this venture. I am in my home office and can see spring arriving in my yard here in central Missouri from a window near my desk.

I hope the Divine Presence is with me as I get back to writing tomorrow or the day after. I need to leave my author world and get to my housewife duty of emptying the dryer.

# The Birth, the Loss

*I have managed to open my laptop again and write an outline. My typing pauses. Do I want to start with one of the darkest days in this story, the birth of my child that would be given away?*

*Lord, give me strength and clarity, among other things.*

It was a beautiful spring day in 1969, and I vaguely remember feeling very warm as we approached the emergency room doors. I was scheduled for induced labor. I'm not sure I needed the induced part. Bruce, my best friend Diane's fiancé and a good friend to me as well, wheeled me into the emergency room. I felt increasingly hot and sweaty. One of the nursing staff asked Bruce if he was my husband.

My story at work as an RN on a pediatric unit across town from the hospital where I would give birth was that I had already separated from my husband after a brief marriage, and he was serving in the army in Viet Nam. Not sure why I didn't go ahead and say I was a widow, but that would have gotten too much attention and sympathy, perhaps.

The nursing staff on the obstetric floor I was entering didn't engage me in happy banter. One of them said, "I bet you'll be glad when this is all over." My chart documented that I was part of the "NO SHOW, NO TELL" protocol. This meant that the baby wasn't to be shown from the nursery window and nothing about the birth was to be told outside the hospital staff. I was also included in this protocol of silence even though I was the mother. I would not be told much about the baby I was having.

A nurse started an IV in my arm after giving me a Brazilian version of the hospital pre-delivery shave and wash. I was essentially a sheep going to slaughter, meek and mild and submissive to what must be done. I don't recall talking with my OB doctor about the NO SHOW NO TELL protocol before the delivery. Still, afterward, at the first postpartum visit, he explained that it would make it easier for me not to see my baby or to know much about it.

I will always wonder if I had had this chance to see her, would I have been able to go through with it, the giving away part? To this day, I greatly regret not seeing or holding her. At least I would have had that chance to look into her eyes, examine her perfect body, count her fingers and toes, and maybe tell her I was sorry that I couldn't be her forever mommy.

Before delivery, I was given a combination of drugs that blocked my memory. So I don't remember the beautiful tiny baby weighing only five pounds and 15 ounces. In later years my friend Diane who was with me in delivery, told me that she had thought I knew my baby's sex and that she was a lovely baby with a full head of dark, curly hair.

After I gave birth and was taken to my private room on the postpartum floor, I woke up sometime in the middle of the night to a dark room. I felt my tummy. It was smaller, although not completely flat. I remember reaching for the phone I knew was on my bedside table. I called Diane, not realizing she needed to sleep after being in the delivery room for hours with me. She sounded groggy when she answered. I think I asked her if I'd had the baby. She was reassuring that, indeed, I had. I think I asked if the baby was normal. I didn't ask about the sex, following the preplanned protocol of not knowing much of anything.

What I do remember distinctly was feeling a profound loss and deep sadness. I wasn't prepared for this. Had it not been a private adoption, handled through the doctor and a lawyer representing the adoptive family, I might have had some counseling from an agency social worker or someone else trained in the needs of birth mothers. In the 60s, when Rose Diane was born, birth mothers often got some needed emotional preparation before and after the birth through the social service agencies who handled the adoption. But I did not.

I started grieving in earnest while in my hospital room. I cried endlessly, it seemed. Of course, I heard babies crying, too, as they were brought from the nursery to their mothers' rooms nearby for feedings. They were crying due to hunger. I, too, was crying due to hunger, but an emotional hunger, not physical.

One day one of the nurses stood silently but respectfully at my bedside as I wept, a witness to my sorrow. It seemed that she stood there for five, maybe 10 whole minutes. She never spoke. Nor did I. I have thought about that nurse for years and wish to thank her for doing that. She recognized my grief and honored it in her silent witness.

Nonetheless, I kind of wonder why she didn't speak. Maybe she could have asked, "Are you sure this is what you want to do? Is there someone you'd like to speak to about it?" No doubt she felt restricted by the plan of a prominent physician who would have been upset if anyone interfered with providing a baby to an infertile "deserving" couple who had sought him out to get a newborn to adopt.

In contrast to birth mothers who had professional social workers, my counseling consisted of the judge and lawyer giving me some terse advice in the judge's private chambers four days after delivery. I had gone there with the adoptive parents' lawyer to sign away my rights.

"It's OK that this happened once, but don't let it happen a second time," one of them said to me, quickly followed by something like, "Yes, one time is okay, but not a second time," by the other. How consoling was that? I recall weeping through most of the signing.

Were they oblivious? Did they think this would be helpful? I have never even remotely understood this advice from these two imposing men of authority. I remember thinking, "Why would they care? It would be more business for them if it happened again." But had it happened that I carelessly got pregnant a second time without being married, I would hope that I would not have chosen to give another child to strangers.

# Childhood Memories and why
# I am the way I Became

I need to understand why I am the way I became and relate this to my ability to give away my child. Maybe it's only making excuses for a mistake I shouldn't have made, maybe a justifiable defense. In any case, I will try to share what I think contributed to my becoming a birth mother later.

I was the youngest in a Catholic family of eight children in a small town in central Missouri. The church up the street was a big part of our lives along with its teachings and practices of prayer and attending Mass and other services frequently.

Following religious and family rules were strongly enforced at home and reinforced by the Catholic nuns who taught me in grade school.

Our family's home life had a predictable rhythm, with firm parental guidance in almost everything, especially what occurred within the walls of our home. We were allowed to play outside and ride our bikes all over town and sometimes into the countryside, a mere block away. We played with neighbor kids and friends from school in the street in front of our house, in backyards, and the Catholic school playgrounds without supervision. It was a relatively carefree and happy childhood.

At home, I can't recall my mother not having the radio on in the kitchen corner when she was preparing a meal, canning, or baking a dessert; all activities kept her in the kitchen quite a lot. As a young child, I often played at the kitchen table with the radio only a few inches away. It was usually tuned to a local station about 13 miles away in the next town.

Ted B. was the daytime radio announcer, and everybody around knew his voice. He read the admissions and discharges from the hospital, births, deaths, arrests, and other news. There was a call-in show when people in the audience wished friends and family a happy birthday. One show provided people a way to advertise items for sale, a small-town radio version of today's eBay.

*Judith - 1955*

*At age seven I stand next to a stroller containing one of many beloved dolls I mothered throughout my early childhood.*

One day I tried to write a story about a bear, complete with drawings. It was mainly plagiarized from a children's book I had recently read. "Mom, look at the book I wrote," I said, hoping to get her praise. She looked at my childish prose and drawings, and I recall that she didn't seem too impressed. She was obviously in the middle of something and could not muster up much enthusiasm. "That's nice," she said distractedly.

At some point, the news came on. Ted B. was talking about someone who had gotten into some sort of trouble. "The unmarried mother ..." he said, as part of the report about the woman. I thought about this phrase for a while and asked my mother, "How can someone be a mother and not be married?" Now I had her attention. She only briefly stopped what she was doing and responded with words I have never forgotten. I don't think she turned away from the sink. "When she sins," she said and resumed her task without further explanation. The apparent conclusion was that having a baby without marriage made the woman a sinner. I didn't ask what that sin might be, but I figured it out years later.

I was not too fond of Saturdays as a kid. It was my job for a long time to clean the bathroom, the only one in the house until Dad had a toilet with a wooden stall installed in the concrete-floored basement. My cleaning regimen consisted of using Comet on the sink, countertop, and tub, scrubbing it, and rinsing. I am pretty sure I used toilet bowl cleaner where it was needed. Not enjoying this job, I would drag it out so long that my siblings would complain that I needed to finish so they could use the bathroom. I never remember Mom complaining. I'm sure she didn't want to discourage any help she could get.

Then in the afternoon, we marched up the street for Saturday confessions, where we waited in line outside the confessional to tell the priest our sins. We would examine our conscience kneeling in the pews just outside the confessional. Sometimes you could almost hear what the priest and currently confessing penitent said if their voices were loud enough. I don't recall really hearing anything scandalous. I remember the dread and anxiety I felt before taking my turn telling my sins and seeking sacramental absolution. Most of my sins were disobeying my parents and fighting with my sisters. Later in life, these confessions might have become much juicier, although I don't really remember any specifics.

When I was in my early grade school years at the nearby parochial school taught by nuns, I recall being especially proud of my sister Barbara. She had joined the Benedictine convent where these teaching nuns originated. One day at recess, while the other kids were on the playground, I drew an image of my sister in her habit, the black and white outfit all the nuns in her order wore at that time. I tried to draw the starched, pleated white collar framing her face and the long black garment that covered most of her body. I wrote her name alongside the image. My teacher let it stay on the board for several days. No one said anything about it to me. I guess I was being boastful. Maybe I should have confessed that.

During my early childhood, one of my sisters and my mom had terrible, loud arguments in our home from time to time. I remember being negatively affected and somewhat terrified when this happened. Through the years, this sister would have periods of severe depression and periods of high energy, along with odd, sometimes embarrassing behavior in public. Hence, Mom and Dad were advised to send her for inpatient psychiatric treatment. At a state mental hospital, she apparently had a new procedure of that time called insulin shock therapy to try to help her. She told me once that it was terrible, and she felt angry that our parents had subjected her to such an awful experience. In later years she got on medication for bipolar illness. In her early life and onto the present day, she has a loving heart and a spontaneous, cheerful personality. Her moods have been stable for many years, and she is enjoying her golden years enriched with many friends, two sons, and several grandchildren. She and I like going out to lunch regularly.

But my sister's bipolar illness had a significant impact on my life. I remember trying to speak my mind to my mother occasionally and being cut off quickly with, "Don't talk back. You don't want to be like your sister, do you?" That placed a roadblock into any personality development toward an assertive nature. Unfortunately, this often-repeated rebuke left me with a rather meek, compliant attitude toward anyone who seemed to be in a dominant position over me. To this day, I have trouble expressing my needs or dealing with anger or disagreements.

The exception to this was apparent in my relationships with my siblings, who I no doubt considered my equals. If I wanted to do some activity or chore, such as hanging up clothes on the line in our backyard, I had my own ideas of how this should be done. I protested against my older sister's instructions, saying, "If I can't do it my way, I just won't do it at all," my sister told me I had said. Mom backed me up by telling her through the kitchen window that looked out to the backyard that she'd better let Judy do it her way, or she wouldn't get Judy's help. So I was a bit strong-willed and maybe a bit spoiled, one might surmise when I felt safe having my own way.

By the time I got to high school, I was generally a rule follower, probably a brown-noser, who made excellent grades and caused no problems for teachers or my parents. But I managed to break a few rules here and there, but usually under the radar of authority figures.

I was a freshman at the small-town public high school when a scandal rocked the town. Two girls in the sophomore class got pregnant at about the same time. Both the girls and the boys they were dating were from upstanding families. It was shocking and a massive deal at the time. The principal called an all-school assembly for the entire high school student body and spoke about the issue. It seemed to me that the girls suffered the most from being looked down on for this social infraction. One of the girls was absent from school for a week, and the other married her boyfriend and had a baby. Her family moved to another town shortly after. None of this was lost on me. Unwed pregnancy was a big deal. It provoked community condemnation and social banishment.

Maybe partially related, I was sent to a boarding school the following year. In hindsight, I believe it was my parents' efforts to protect me from a similar fate that these two girls and their families experienced.

My sister Barbara was just up the hill from the boarding school in the Benedictine sisters' convent along with another sister, Berniece, who had entered what was referred to as the Aspirancy there. Berniece "aspired" to be a nun and entered right after grade school, as most nuns had at that time.

I think my parents assumed I would see my two sisters regularly, but this was not what happened. We would have short visits together on the weekends, but our lives were mainly separate. My sisters lived a life of spirituality and study in a picturesque building of Gothic Revival design. It was separate from the boarding school, but a short walk away and up a concrete pathway to a more modern brick building with classrooms, dormitories, a cafeteria, and a chapel. My life was suddenly one of trying to adjust to a highly competitive private school of predominantly Catholic girls. Day students from the city of Fort Smith also attended.

In a large dorm containing maybe a dozen or more single beds and bedside tables, I cried every night that first year. I felt friendless in a foreign world. The other girls who had started as freshmen a year earlier had their friends already, and neither they nor I made much effort to include me.

I endured my loneliness mostly in silence. I didn't tell anyone in my family that I was dreadfully homesick. Letters went back and forth between my friends and me in Missouri and my parents. It was a relief not to be around the discord between my oldest sister and my mother. However, I felt an acute loss of much-needed familiarity and closeness with my family, hometown friends, and the town where I had spent the first 14 years of my life.

I would go home at Thanksgiving, Christmas, and Easter break, but otherwise didn't leave the school grounds with two exceptions. One was being allowed to go to downtown Fort Smith on Saturdays. The other was overnight visits to other students' homes if I had special written parental permission to visit.

We were assigned a Prefect, who was a nun from the convent, and had an office and bedroom adjacent to our dormitories. She would call girls into her office who needed redirection or discussions about their behavior, grades, activities, etc. She read our letters before being sent out in the regular mail. I recall being advised that one of my letters was not to be sent because there were disparaging remarks about the nuns or the school, but I don't recall which. My mother told me that one time she got a letter from the Prefect saying they were concerned about how I danced at one of the dances we had with the Subiaco boys. She seemed to find this more amusing than concerning, to my delight and amazement.

Occasionally the priests and nuns collaborated to hold dances for the boys from Subiaco and girls from St. Scholastica in our large recreation room with live bands who played current rock and roll hits. Like St. Scholastica, Subiaco was a monastery with a boarding school, but for boys. It was run by Benedictine priests in a small town, Subiaco, about 50 miles south. Ironically my father had spent a short time there, about six months, as a high school student before he succumbed to homesickness and returned home to Pilot Grove. He'd been thinking about becoming a Catholic priest and joining the monastery there. In those days when he was a boy, there were even fewer trips home during the school year.

During my second year at boarding school, I acquired a boyfriend who went to Subiaco. We were one of the few brave couples who danced fast dances, so our movements could be more easily seen than the more crowded slow dances. I don't recall precisely what the chaperoning nun might have seen as objectionable, but I never got a reprimand from my parents. Efforts to keep me chaste were successful, as my physical contact with boys at school was limited to dancing and later quick kisses at the door, all under a nun's surveillance.

My contact with boys on dates at home was not as monitored but was usually limited to double dates with another couple. It wasn't that I didn't have the opportunity to be more sexually active, but I purposefully maintained my virgin status all through high school.

I recall one double date with a football player from the University of Missouri. It was a blind date arranged by one of my hometown girlfriends and her boyfriend, who went to college there. I remember sitting in the backseat with him in a parked car in the driveway of my home with my girlfriend and her boyfriend in the front seat. I think we had been to the movies in nearby Boonville, and it was time to say goodnight and goodbye.

Neither my date nor I seemed too interested in each other, and we had little conversation all evening. This didn't stop the big young fellow next to me from initiating a long kiss in which he proceeded to put his tongue in my mouth. Don't get me wrong. I had nothing against kissing, even on a first date. But, I had never before French kissed, only having heard about it from priests and nuns in the context of it being a sin. I didn't like this invasion into my body in such an intimate way by someone I hardly knew and didn't particularly like. So I did what any good Catholic girl should do. I bit his tongue. This, of course, had an immediate response from the poor guy as he pulled away and held his mouth in a way that registered pain. I think our night out soon ended then, although I don't recall whether or not my tongue-impaired date walked me to the door or not. Probably not.

Shortly after this unfortunate event, I heard from my girlfriend that I'd made quite an impression, not positive, on my date and my girlfriend's boyfriend. Word got around because I was subsequently asked out by the brother of my girlfriend's boyfriend, who told me he thought it was great that I'd bitten the tongue of the big football player. We hit it off, double-dated, and went "steady" for about a year or so during part of my high school years.

# Other Losses and Detachments

I seem to have in my personality makeup the ability, or tendency at least, to be emotionally numb or detached at times. This is perhaps beneficial to some degree and not uncommon in others; however, I think I have an overabundance.

I recall making a conscious choice not to feel anything during periods of anxiety when others around me were upset early in my grade school years. This tendency to emotionally detach me figured into my pregnancy significantly. I had decided not to keep my baby early on, so I didn't let myself become attached to her. I surmised that this would protect me from the potential loss after her birth. Other previous losses prepared me for this as well.

My first time of loss, no doubt, occurred shortly after I was born. I was the ninth child born to my parents. The first had died shortly after birth due to complications during cesarean delivery. Mom had almost died after giving birth to her firstborn, Theresa. Mom's blood pressure had been out of control. But subsequent pregnancies were uncomplicated, so uneventful that home deliveries were possible for two of my siblings.

But mine was a hospital birth. Mother brought me home and was immediately confronted with a houseful of children and an exhausted mother-in-law who had taken care of us during her absence. Grandma had been cooking, cleaning, and minding the children well, no doubt, but was anxious to return home and leave soon after Mom arrived. Dad didn't cook, nor did he do the day-to-day household management that was traditionally a woman's role at that time.

With a new baby, seven children under 15 years old, cooking, laundry, and so forth, Mom had a "nervous breakdown," she explained to me many years later. Also, during this time, she suffered from severely infected gums and teeth, requiring full extraction and dentures. No doubt this contributed a lot toward my mother's nervous breakdown. Who wouldn't have one with all this going on?

Her doctor recommended a return to the hospital for postpartum rest. We children, except for my oldest brother, were parceled out to live temporarily with relatives. I went to my godparents' home. When they brought me back, the family story was that I had gained so much weight that mom said, "Your cow must have given delicious milk." I would presume by that comment that I was given cow's milk rather than formula had it even been available in 1947. I still like milk and often prefer it to other options. After Mom returned home, the extra help from teen cousins and other hired help was called to assist with childcare and household chores.

I have wondered what effect my mother's absence had on my infant psyche. I think psychologists would say I had feelings of abandonment because of it. Even though I thrived physically, as evidenced by my weight gain, I possibly suffered from missing my mommy, the being who had been attached to me for the previous nine months. Aunt Nellie, my godmother and mom's sister, indeed had similar physical characteristics, but she wasn't mom.

Subsequent instances of loss involved pet cats.

We had a cat named Boots who regularly became pregnant with a litter of kittens.

Generally, pets were not allowed in our house, but when she went into labor (and how this was discerned, I couldn't say), she was granted the privilege of having a spot in a lined basket at the bottom of the stairs in the basement. After Boots gave birth, probably a couple of weeks or more later, she and the kittens were returned to the outside and found refuge from the elements and predators underneath the back porch.

We would play with the kittens for a few weeks, but they would mysteriously be gone without a trace. I don't recall being particularly upset about it, and in my early years might not have even noticed they were gone for several days. It became common knowledge that Dad had taken the successive litters of kittens in a gunny sack out to the local creek, where they met their early deaths. Boots was allowed to live and probably kept the local mouse population at bay. Having her surgically fixed to prevent this periodic event was no doubt not in our thrifty family's budget or cultural practice.

Once in a while, I was allowed to keep one of the kittens. I recall playing with one in the backyard and giving her affection, treats of hot dog pieces, feeding her, and filling a water bowl. I don't recall how often it happened, but more than once, my growing kitten would become lethargic and stop eating. Because our cats didn't have the benefit of a veterinarian to give them shots, they likely died of feline leukemia or some other disease. Perhaps they ingested poison from somewhere. I hope it wasn't at my father's hands, but considering his record with the gunny sack, I sometimes wonder.

I recall feeling anxious when I noticed the latest object of my pet-parenting love getting ill and hoping it wouldn't die as the last one had. I am not sure how these repeated losses of my cats affected me, but I doubt if it was healthy. I was always ready to love the next kitten I was allowed to raise for a few months.

Then there were the upsetting periodic blowups in our home between my sister and mother. Whatever prompted these, such as mom correcting her, wanting her to do something she didn't want to do, or other disagreements, my sister would yell loudly and angrily at my mother. Sometimes it seemed she was screaming and running through our house, passing me on her way to the kitchen as she had it out with mom. I recall these happening with some regularity, and it left me frightened and upset. I vowed that I never wanted to display such anger and would not let myself get upset about things that might typically upset a young girl.

My two sisters, closest in age to me, sometimes wanted to involve me in their disagreements. I generally chose to stay aloof. I didn't want to be part of an argument or display anger like that, which upset me. It wasn't until I was well into my middle years that the concept of assertiveness and the desire to be assertive rather than passive or aggressive entered my vocabulary. My choice to get a job as a psychiatric nurse figured into my goal to learn about some of the unhealthy behavior in myself and others in my family, especially my sister, who had high irritability and mood swings.

Another loss that I grieved during childhood that might have contributed to my growing shell of non-emotion involved my dog, Teddy. From time to time, over the years, we had dogs for pets, and they were always relegated to living outside and roaming free, as I recall. In our small town, there were no regulations that prohibited this. I don't remember clearly having dog houses for them, but they had the space under the porch to avoid the rain and snow.

Teddy was a cute and playful brown and white puppy when I got him. He was my dog. I must have been around nine or 10 at the time. I don't know what breed he was; he was mixed by whatever stray romanced his mother. I kept a small diary that I read later in my adulthood that logged, "I played with the dog today," day after day for months.

Teddy was a cute puppy, but his aggressive playfulness worried my mom as he grew in size. One day he bit me on my face. It wasn't enough to cause bleeding or even bite marks, I don't think, but it scared me, and I sat on the back porch steps crying. Mom came out to do something, possibly to put some wet clothes on the lines and asked me what was wrong.

"Teddy bit me," I moaned through my tears.

Teddy disappeared shortly after that, maybe a few days or weeks. When I reported her missing to my parents, they told me that some men had come to take her to a farm where she could be of use as a farm dog. Despite this explanation to appease me, I envisioned Teddy baring her teeth and growling as several men approached her with a rope. Then I ran into the bathroom, locked the door, and wailed loudly so the whole household could hear me. I displayed significant emotion for quite some time in that small room. So much for me being above emotional feelings. My grief and loss of Teddy was a precursor to my later early but temporary display of grief in my early twenties after giving birth to Rose.

Dad started talking to me outside the locked door, encouraging me to come out. I think he talked about the benefits of Teddy helping the farmer out by herding his cattle and keeping them from straying, but a bribe of a quarter finally convinced me to unlock the door.

That could buy a lot of penny candy at Beau Warnhoff's candy counter downtown.

I understand my parents' decision to remove a clear danger from their child, but perhaps some preparation would have been less traumatic for me. That I was so easily comforted by a quarter is somewhat sad, but the fact that daddy was taking the time to talk to me and offer some sort of peace offering was compensation enough.

*I got my very own puppy, Teddy, when I was nine years old.*

I don't recall getting any consoling hug from either parent due to Teddy's loss. Their German ancestry did not culturally include much physical hugging and affection toward us children. In later life, this changed some with some hand-holding and "I love you" declarations, especially when my mother was in her last year.

As I described earlier, going away to a boarding school at the age of 15 was a stressful time for me. I recall feeling incredibly lonely and without close friends the first year. My two sisters lived close by in the monastic part of the St. Scholastica complex, but they might as well have been in the next county.

The Sunday visits we had were totally unlike the family or childhood times at home. No Sunday dinner shared with my siblings and frequent visiting relatives, no hikes out to Coon Creek or games of cards and monopoly. I don't remember our visits because they were unmemorable and emotionally unfulfilling. This is not a criticism of my sisters, who were, and are, wonderful people and enjoyable companions. It was just not a home-like atmosphere; the world they lived in was full of scheduled prayer times and classes held apart from my school and dormitory life at the academy only yards away.

Already I tended to tolerate unhappiness at times. I knew my parents wanted me to get a Catholic high school experience away from the dangers of teenage life in our small-town public school. I persevered with nearly constant studying to keep up my grades. I comforted myself during my nightly tearfulness with spoons of peanut butter stashed on my bedside table. My pattern of denying my own need for happiness was already part of my ongoing personal experience.

I don't think I thought I had a choice to come back home that first year. However, I was assertive enough during the summer of my first school year away at boarding school to tell my parents that I wanted to stay home. Not thinking my wish would make any difference anyway, I accepted a portable radio they offered under the condition I return to the academy. I was bought by a paltry bribe yet again. I accepted, feeling temporarily powerful and in the position of being persuaded rather than commanded.

Fortunately, the following year I became friends with several girls at boarding school who are still friends. Although I did express the desire to stay home again for my senior year, I returned to the academy partly to continue being with my friends. If I had stayed home, my other choice would have been to attend the Catholic high school in a neighboring town. I sometimes wonder how my life would have been different had I chosen this option. I strongly suspect I might have dated and married a local boy and perhaps avoided my untimely pregnancy.

My ability to detach myself from feeling loss or simply tolerating unhappiness figured into my mindset and coping during my pregnancy with Rose. I loved children and enjoyed being around my nieces and nephews from infancy through childhood. I dreamed of being married and having a house full of kids, but at the time of my first pregnancy, I could deny what I truly wanted.

*My childhood home had two small bedrooms downstairs and one large one upstairs, housing eight children and our parents.*

# Emotional Numbness

For many, it must seem unimaginable not to have some sort of emotional bond with a baby growing inside your own body. But my ability to detach was the critical ingredient in my ability to place her for adoption. I didn't deny the pregnancy was happening. I made the conscious effort to think of it as a temporary condition, which it certainly was, and that this child would be going to a couple waiting for a baby.

As I've described, I'd had practice dealing with challenging emotions or not really dealing with them.

At boarding school, I felt homesick and depressed sometimes, but I kept pretty busy studying to keep the grades I expected of myself and pushed my sadness aside as best I could.

I dealt with disappointment at not enjoying nursing school as much as my friends did by attending the rigorous program and keeping busy with coursework and clinical practice. There were good times to be sure, with my friends and dating relationships, but I didn't really enjoy studying nursing. One of my freshman instructors said, "You don't enjoy nursing much, do you?" I denied it and said I did, not wanting to rock the boat or not finish what I had started, perhaps. I could have insisted on leaving nursing school but didn't think of any alternative paths. I was familiar with denying negative or painful feelings or just tolerating them.

Additionally, as a young student in a Catholic grade school, the concept of offering up suffering for the poor souls in purgatory gave the definite message that suffering could be helpful. It was to be endured and even expected. As a female in a male-dominated society and raised in a family where talking back was promptly discouraged,

I didn't complain or voice my opinion much, nor did I have the verbal skills to express dissatisfaction or anger acceptably except to a few friends.

I realize I don't present much of a healthy or happy version of myself. I was told by more than one counselor that I was dysthymic, tending toward depression, which is often the result of anger held inward.

During my pregnancy, I recall being fascinated when Rose started to move. But I never talked to her or sang as many pregnant women do to their newborns. I didn't allow myself to feel love for her or feel pleasure related to my motherhood. This was a situation that I needed to suffer through, and then it would be over. She would be taken away and given to a family consisting of a married man and woman that a trusted doctor had approved. She was spoken for and not indeed my child, I consciously thought.

I did what I needed to stay healthy by eating well and not participating in dangerous activities or unusual physical adventures that would have jeopardized my bodily well-being. However, I may have drunk alcohol to excess on at least two occasions during the pregnancy, and I am sorry for this. Either I ignored the medical recommendations against this, or they had not been as emphasized as they are to pregnant women today.

I was concerned that the baby was healthy. If she had deformities or some condition that required lots of medical intervention, the adoption might not happen. Then I would have a whole new set of problems. I recall thinking about this rather unemotionally; I am ashamed to admit it.

It was more like a business deal that might be canceled than a poor, tiny baby who needed help and a mother who would take care of her. It was a complication I didn't want to have to happen.

I've often wondered if Rose Diane ever felt a longing for me or any loss when we were separated at her birth. I had not talked or sung to her in my tummy as I have learned many expectant mothers, even other prospective birth moms, often did. I didn't have counseling from the doctor or anyone in the medical profession about preparing myself for the separation.

One would think medical and nursing schools would have had protocols or best practices within their programs to help birth mothers with their emotional needs. Perhaps this has changed since the 1960s.

I have read and heard of many birth mothers who did bond with their babies, got to hold them after birth, spent time with them, and bonded. Many pregnant women talk, sing, and allow a complete emotional experience with the growing being inside them. I understand that babies know the rhythms, voices, and other biological factors unique to their mother that they sense within the womb.

For the mothers who bonded this way, I am sure their last time together with their babies was excruciatingly painful. These are well documented in numerous books and articles about birth mothers. There are many sad accounts written by birth mothers and in live personal presentations at adoption conferences that I eventually attended. I was spared this devastation. I surmise this was part of the reason for not allowing me to see my baby. But still … I would have endured it and been better off in the long run.

I was a relatively thin person at 117 pounds at the pregnancy's beginning and produced a tiny newborn who weighed a mere five pounds and 15 ounces. The doctor told me the baby was healthy, which was pleasing and relieving. I had always liked the small five-pounders in the nursery during my obstetric rotation in nursing school. I was relieved because her adoption would more likely proceed without complications that might occur if she were not healthy. I was not alarmed by her low birth weight, which I knew was still in the normal range.

Did my detachment and lack of bonding with my unborn child cause a matching aloofness on the part of infant Rose Diane? When she was put in the waiting and joyful arms of her new parents, she possibly felt, for the first time, an acceptance and love she had not previously sensed while in the womb. I feel I missed an excellent opportunity with Rose that can never be recaptured. Would the adult Rose need to renew a relationship or bond she once felt with me?

Of course, I regret that I chose to detach from my unborn child. I not only missed the opportunity to share a mother-child bond while she was in my uterus but also for the loss it might have cost me in my efforts to form an adult relationship with her later.

Through the years, I had read and heard countless stories of the instant recognition mothers saw in their newborns' faces when they looked into their eyes and spoke or sang to them shortly after birth. Numerous studies report that newborns will follow their mother's voice by turning their heads toward her as she moves around in a room they are both in. Rose no doubt heard my voice during her formation within me. Still, it was not directed toward her in a loving and soothing tone; hence, I feel immense regret about this.

# More About Boarding School

When I went away to boarding school over 300 miles away from my Missouri hometown, letters were extremely important to me. I recall spending lots of time picking out delicate stationery at one of the downtown department stores on the occasional times I ventured off campus with other boarders.

We were allowed to leave the dorm to shop downtown on Saturdays. It was a highlight of the week for me. I didn't dread Saturdays as I had back home when I had to clean the family bathroom and later tell my sins in the confessional at our church up the street.

Several other boarders and I would walk about two miles down Rogers Avenue to get to the downtown area. I no longer remember the name of my favorite department store, but I spent a lot of time looking at merchandise with my friends. I bought some clothes there during my senior year, but mainly just bought stationery.

Onion skin paper was my favorite, with its thin, delicate paper and pale colors, sometimes even scented. Not only did we write to our parents and friends back home, but if we had a boyfriend at the Catholic boys' boarding school about 50 miles away, that was the usual method of communication at the time. There were no phones readily available to us for regular use.

After classes, we could go to the canteen for soda and snacks. I always liked frozen Dr. Peppers. I'm not sure how it was accomplished that we could enjoy slushy DPs, but I think it was just a matter of taking them out of the canteen freezer and uncapping the bottle. My recollection of the canteen is pleasant. We'd enjoy our sodas and chips, sit in sturdy wooden booths, and chat. Two of the really popular girls from my class worked off some of their tuition by working there during the time I frequented the place. I'm not sure why I didn't work off some of my tuition, but if my parents ever wanted me to, they never expressed it. I hadn't volunteered either.

I remember the recreation room much better. It was a large, square-pillared room with fluorescent lighting, concrete block walls and linoleum tiles. There was a jukebox with current hits from the sixties that we could play without inserting any coins. I recall practicing the popular dances to Beatles favorites with some of my girlfriends.

The first year I was just a homesick, lonely small-town girl, totally out of her element in an institution of nuns and girls, studying my head off to keep the good grades I had always expected of myself. Returning the fall after that first year, I displayed a framed 8x10 of my hometown summer boyfriend and soon was finally accepted by several of my classmates. If I could put a cute guy's picture on my bedside stand, there must be something interesting or cool about me, apparently.

My friends or upper classmates fixed me up with a couple of boys from Subiaco for a couple of dance dates. One of them, named Joe, was tall and nice looking, as I recall, but neither of us knew how to carry on a conversation. We spent an entire awkward evening saying a few words and dancing a few slow dances to the live band the nuns had hired. This relationship fizzled before it got started.

I was honored to be invited to the prom at St. Anne's Catholic High School in town by the brother of one of the popular day students, another arranged fixup. I was somewhat intimidated when our names were announced to all attending as we entered the large gymnasium, given all the other prom goers. This very nice and gentlemanly boy and I had little to say to each other just like all the other dates so far

28

during my boarding school days. We had no common experiences, and I admit my social skills were poorly developed, so I take what blame there is for my half of the silent dates. Although this boy asked me out again, I didn't see much future in it, so I declined.

But my social life with the opposite sex improved when a cute boy named Kevin and I found each other at one of the dances. He was a year younger, but a good dancer who would dance fast dances with me. We wrote to each other between dances and apparently had enough to say in the letters or in person at the infrequent social events the nuns and the priests at Subiaco collaborated on. But our love for dancing and the rock music of the time was the main attraction; plus, Kevin had a Beatles-type haircut and looked cool in his Subiaco blue blazer. We were considered a couple.

I don't recall going to many of Subiaco's football games, but we did have a cheerleading squad that went to them from our school. One of my best friends was a cheerleader and more in the true "in-crowd" of the social scene than I. I remember feeling like I was missing out on high school fun. Going home on Thanksgiving, Christmas and Easter holidays, sometimes by train, was a time to make up for lost time and experiences of normal teen life. I had no qualms about dating other boys besides Kevin while at home for the holidays. I had my home life in Pilot Grove and my sparse social life in Arkansas.

The train rides to and from Kansas City Union Station were fun. Sometimes I'd bring home a friend from school. One year we went up and down the aisles of the train car selling the big chocolate nut candy bars for 50 cents each as a fundraiser for the academy. Another year I had scavenged some alcohol from the top cabinet in the kitchen at home into tiny bottles that we emptied into our sodas for the trip back to Arkansas. Apparently, this moral infraction made it into the rumor mills of the academy upon our return, and I was called on the carpet by one of the more straight-laced day students for this behavior.

Along with friends who came home with me, I would double date during school vacations. Friends of my dates were paired with my visiting friends. One of the more memorable dates was at a Thursday Holy Week service that mom strongly encouraged us to attend. Our dates, Catholic boys, managed to keep us in stitches during most of the otherwise solemn services instead of concentrating on praying. They did such things as getting the handheld candles to stick to the backrest of the pew in front of us while the candles were still lit. This act seems scandalous now, rather sacrilegious, but at the time, it was hilarious to us teens.

Our family gatherings revolved around a big meal cooked mostly by my mother with help from the females in the family, mainly my sisters-in-law. We daughters didn't help in the kitchen much at family dinners because this area was Mom's domain, and we really didn't do much except set the table with dinnerware or maybe mash potatoes at times.

Family get-togethers were generally happy times involving playing with the grandkids, holding new babies, eating big turkeys, and delicious pies, Christmas trees, presents, and teasing brothers. It also included attendance at church services and praying the rosary each night with whoever was at home at the time.

In retrospect, I think my boarding school experience was fairly positive. Besides making some good life-long friends, I got a good education in preparation for college. I also got a firm foundation for a belief in furthering social justice issues, for which the Benedictine nuns can take much of the credit. But still, I felt I was missing out on the normal fun of school life at home.

I recall going to Little Rock along with some of the nuns and participating in a march on the streets there in favor of civil rights for black people. Once I wrote a paper in which I stated the Catholic Church had no history of racial discrimination. My English teacher wrote on the paper that this was not a true statement, which made me question assumptions and to get evidence for my beliefs.

I don't mean to brag, but I generally never had a shortage of boys who wanted to date me, at least in my youth. Time at home was short and packed with dates and family holiday gatherings. Too soon, I had to return to hard studying, strict rules, restricted activities, and scheduled institutional life.

In addition to forming my moral and political principles, I think boarding school broadened my worldview and made me more adventurous in many ways. Oh yes, it may also have helped prevent me from getting pregnant during my high school years.

# Josh, the Party Animal

After the regimented life at a boarding school, I found myself in a less restrictive living environment in a three-year nursing school run by Mercy nuns in Springfield, Missouri, with fewer limits to our comings and goings at the dormitory compared to boarding school.

Fortunately, I was at least closer to home, with only a three-hour drive. I relied on catching rides home with a guy from my hometown who worked in Springfield until I got my first car in the spring of my senior year.

I lived in a dorm of mostly single rooms with other female nursing students and was expected to follow a set of behavior rules involving demerits for rule infractions. An office person at the main desk on the first floor observed our comings and goings, but the surveillance of our behavior was minimal. I recall signing in and out at the desk in the lobby reception area whenever I left campus. Not having a car, I depended on friends who did, or my dates, to drive me anywhere off campus. We had science classes at the state college across town during our freshman year.

Because we didn't have much of a summer break and only a few more trips home than when I was at St. Scholastica's, my boyfriends at home became less of a factor in my life. I began dating and got engaged to a cute fraternity guy named Erick. We were in a very close and eventually intimate relationship for about a year and a half. I broke it off and gave back the engagement ring when he suddenly dropped out of college and took a job as a portrait photographer traveling from one J. C. Penney to another throughout the Midwest. I had thought I was in love, but I couldn't see myself marrying someone who didn't have a college degree, plus his sudden absence without letters and frequent phone calls dampened my ardor. I am fortunate that a pregnancy did not occur with Erick, although I probably would have married him if he had been willing.

I completed nursing school and passed the Missouri Board exams to become a registered nurse, which undoubtedly pleased my parents and made my future more economically secure.

Along came Josh in my final months of school. We'd seen each other in the hospital. He was working his way through college by working as an orderly there. He was very good-looking, and I admired him from a distance. He managed to strike up a conversation with me one day on the unit where I was doing my psychiatric clinicals. He didn't have to sell himself too hard to get me to agree to go out with him.

Josh was a party guy with lots of friends. So, when he told me he thought I was the cutest girl in my class, I was flattered and thrilled to be chosen for his attention.

In a short period, we became intimate despite my initial reluctance. With some guilt, I disregarded my own rule about sexual activity. In my rationalization, I should refrain from premarital sex unless I truly felt I loved the guy. But, like the popular song lyrics, what's love got to do with it?

After all, Josh represented a lot of what I had missed in boarding school, namely the typical social avenues young people pursue to have fun. He invited me to dance parties, dining out with groups of his friends, and to swim and boat on a nearby lake. In addition to his good looks, he had a cool convertible and often made me laugh.

"I know you were engaged," he said, telling me he understood I had been sexually active before. Although I initially said no to "going all the way" with him, I submitted to his advances. If I were to do it all over, I would have engaged some backbone, said an emphatic "no!" to his demands and quit dating him. Potentially I would not have had this story to tell.

*The author's nursing school graduation photo taken in 1968*

# Move to Tulsa via Raytown

After graduating from nursing school, I moved my few possessions to Raytown, Missouri, a suburb of Kansas City and shared a studio apartment with a friend from my nursing school class. I got a job in a hospital, my first after officially becoming a registered nurse. My life seemed to spiral downward after Josh visited me and parked his car at my apartment in Raytown before flying to California.

I had left Springfield partly to end my relationship with him because I continued to feel guilty about being sexually active with him outside of marriage. The other reason was to be closer to various family members in the Kansas City area, including three brothers, a sister and numerous nieces and nephews.

At my new job of only a few months, I was beginning to get used to living in a big metropolitan area. I was learning the ropes as a general duty nurse on a medical-surgical unit in a large hospital in Kansas City's famous Plaza area.

Josh visited me in Raytown with little notice, that I recall. After arriving, he suggested I call in sick the next day so we could visit late into the night. Against my better judgment, I agreed to this but with a well-deserved feeling of guilt when I called in sick to work the following morning of a usually low-staffed weekend.

That evening consisted of Josh and I drinking beer and ending up camped out on the floor of the apartment building's party room on the lower level. I became pregnant with Rose Diane that night. I was supremely embarrassed the next morning when the building maintenance guy found Josh and me asleep on the floor. I'm sure he must have reported this to management and probably other tenants who knew me.

Josh left the next day for his trip by plane to visit a friend and have a good time in California. I, on the other hand, got in trouble with the apartment manager while he was gone, not because we had used the party room for our not-so-private boudoir but because Josh had parked his car and left it in a parking spot assigned to someone else. The manager, who was my landlord, was pretty angry. He probably knew about the late-night liaison also but didn't bring it up.

In addition to the trouble in my apartment building, at work, I was indirectly called on the carpet. In a conversation between the head nurse and another nurse in my earshot (probably on purpose), I heard that on the day I called in, supposedly with gastrointestinal problems, only one nurse was left to carry the load of nursing duties that shift and no one was available to replace me. I knew that in the eyes of these sister R.N.s, I was a slacker, and I felt bad about it.

I don't think I heard from Josh again after this visit, and he didn't hear from me until a few months later when I gave him the news by phone that I was pregnant.

It seems our method of birth control failed with reliance on condoms as the only prevention. In my strange thinking, I had an aversion to using the pill, which was, after all, against Catholic doctrine. Using birth control would have meant I planned to have sex outside of marriage, and that planning in itself would have been sinful. "So how convoluted was that?" most rational people would ask. I really hadn't given it much consideration, but in my early twenties, I had the misfortune and common youthful delusion that anything such as pregnancy, death or other great misfortune could not occur in my little world.

Learning about my pregnancy felt like a disaster and unreal. I had my pregnancy test at a laboratory near my apartment building. My roommate learned from the guy she was dating, who knew someone who worked there, that the lab worker had told other people about my pregnancy. This was prior to HIPAA privacy regulations, but profoundly unethical. Possibly the whole apartment building knew about it, including the owner-manager, the maintenance guy, and the really nice nerd who I had stood up for a date, and now maybe my own brother who was friends with the owner-manager. They might as well have put it on the front page of the Kansas City Star.

I was in shock. Now, what was I going to do? I was pregnant by a college playboy who I had tried to stop seeing by moving away, a reflection on me and my avoidant non-assertive personality. I was pretty certain Josh had moved on to his next girlfriend by then. This scenario certainly wasn't evidence of a solid relationship in which you wanted to raise a child.

I never considered abortion. It was illegal in 1968, but at my core, I could not consider killing the life beginning in me, even though I could hardly really believe it was there. It's possible I could have found out somehow how to obtain one. After all, three women of my age confided to me decades later they had gotten abortions during this period while they lived in various areas of the Midwest.

Truly, what was a single, pregnant girl to do in 1968?

I went home one weekend to visit my parents and tell them about my pregnancy. I felt such unbelievable shame. My parents were very religious and loyal Catholics, as were my brothers and sisters, to the best of my knowledge. One of my sisters had been a nun for decades by that time. I had such dread in telling them and so little courage that I didn't, not that weekend nor any subsequent weekend in the next 13 years or so.

The person who I did tell was one of my close friends from nursing school who was living in Tulsa. "What am I going to do?" I frantically asked Diane on the phone. She had known Josh, as did all of my friends and classmates. "Do you want to marry Josh?" she asked.

"Not really," I answered. "He's probably dating someone else by now anyway. We don't love each other." I had always expected to find "Mr. Right," someone I was in love with, just like in all the romantic movies and books I had seen and read.

At some point in the conversation, Diane suggested something that seemed to be a possible option. "What about adoption? There's a doctor here in Tulsa who places babies with really good families." I thought this seemed like a solution that might work for me. At this point, I thought of my pregnancy as a problem, not a baby. She added an enticement. "You could come to Tulsa and room with me. There's room in my apartment. I'm sure you could get a job at the hospital where I work. They're always short of nurses."

Without much further consideration, the escape plan to move to Tulsa and solve the problem with adoption fell into place. I still didn't start thinking of the embryo within my uterus as my child. It was a pregnancy, a problem to solve, not a baby to love, even though immensely inconvenient. I have some sympathy and understanding regarding women and girls who turn to the abortion option to solve their dilemma of unintended pregnancy. Desperate situations often seem to require desperate remedies.

Things moved quickly. I gave notice at my job, which I had only had for about four months. I told my family I was moving to Oklahoma and packed everything I owned at that time in my life into my little blue Volkswagen Beetle. There was just enough room left for my parakeet Foose in her cage on top of some things in the front passenger seat.

My later regrets for this quick decision and flight to Tulsa are several and profound. Had I gone to a social service agency to discuss an adoption plan, it's very likely I would have been educated about the realities of giving up my baby. Some of the realities might have been the grief involved due to the loss I would likely feel. I had no idea this would happen. It is possible, depending on the agency's mission and philosophy, that they would not have counseled me about the likely grief, but reputable and properly trained social workers would have.

For me, it was all an unemotional plan in my head that I needed to carry out. I could go to Oklahoma, have the baby, place him or her for adoption and keep it a secret from my family and continue my life as if it hadn't happened.

Had I had the courage to tell my family, it is entirely possible there would have been an alternative decision. A big part of me believes that my parents might have agreed with the decision about adoption if I truly didn't want to marry the father, but I will never know. In any event, they would have had the chance to be supportive. It would have been a disappointing shock for them, and I'm pretty sure they would not have wanted people and their friends in the small town where I live to know about it.

They probably would have advised me to place the baby with a Catholic social service agency, and she would then have gone to a Catholic family. This factor alone would have been important later because it possibly would have changed her worldview and perhaps established a spiritual kinship. A viewpoint from her evangelical faith suggested that "God's plan for her life" was to be with a different family than mine.

Many years later, I learned that one of my cousins, the same age as me, had placed a baby for adoption when she was 17. My parents might have encouraged me to go to the same Catholic agency she had gone to. My cousin told me that the nuns there were very nice to her.

She was fortunate not to have to keep it a secret from her family and therefore shut them out from the opportunity to help her.

With a due date in early April, I managed to get time off from my job in Tulsa and go to Kansas City for Christmas. I wasn't showing much and was dressed in loose-fitting clothes. My sister-in-law Rita complimented me on a dress I was wearing when I stopped at my brother's house one day. She pulled the pleats apart and looked admiringly at the black and white pilgrim-style dress. I was really afraid she would notice my baby bump, but all she said was, "Oh, what a cute dress."

I was accompanied by an old boyfriend I'd reconnected with at the time. I had divulged my predicament to him, so he knew about my intent to keep it a secret from my family. We caught each other's eyes somewhat fearfully when this near discovery occurred. During that Christmas trip, this same boyfriend offered to marry me and help raise my baby together. I would have married him too. He was from a good Catholic family, and though I liked him a lot, I wasn't madly in love with him. But I thought it might work. I could keep the baby, and somehow things would be fine. So, after all, there was within me a desire to keep my child if only I could be married.

It was a few weeks later after my return to Tulsa that I got a letter from my gallant boyfriend. He apparently had talked it over with someone who counseled him against marrying me. "After you have the baby and place it for adoption, I will marry you," he wrote. However, we did not resume dating after I gave birth and lost touch.

So, it was back to plan A, the adoption plan and keeping it a secret from my family.

# Before and After the Birth

I recall my doctor saying, "I won't be telling you your baby's sex, because if I told you it was a little boy or a little girl, then you might be tempted to think that every child of that sex and age might be yours." I didn't question his obvious lack of logic. So instead of scrutinizing just little boys the approximate age of my child with a genetic resemblance, I would be looking at every child, which would have been twice as many children. Go figure.

Had I been told it was going to be really hard, maybe I would have done it anyway. Suffering was expected per my Catholic religious instruction and my own perception of the human condition. I was surprised, though, at the ferocity of the intense grief I felt in the immediate time after birth, which resurfaced many years later when I woke up from my denial.

As my breasts leaked milk, my eyes leaked tears. My heart was broken. But I had made a decision that was in the process of being carried out. I was not going to stop the train and get off. I felt too much shame. "It was the right thing to do," I told myself, along with, "I can have more children someday when I marry the right man."

Regardless of the emotional trauma I undoubtedly would have had at the time of separation; I wish I had had the opportunity to see and hold my baby. Perhaps I would have instantly fallen in love with her as so many new mothers and fathers do. Perhaps I would not have been able to let her go. I missed that once-in-a-lifetime opportunity.

Additionally, I had been given a combination of drugs during the delivery that blocked any memory of the last part of labor and the birth. I have no recall whatsoever. How much of these drugs and others might have still been in my body four days after delivery when I signed papers put in front of me, I'll never know.

On my first postpartum visit, my doctor told me, "You were quite a tiger." I took that to mean that I was ferocious and actively involved during the delivery. My friend and roommate, Diane, told me later, "You screamed so much and so loud."

It probably hurt like hell, and all the pent up fear and emotion probably came out similar to a fighting tiger. I don't know how my subconscious processed this event, or if it did at all. It is a blank space in my memory.

When Diane and I discussed what the baby looked like at birth many years later, Diane said, "She was a tiny thing, so pretty, with a full head of dark curly hair."

Rose Diane was born healthy at only five pounds and 15 ounces. When I heard the birth weight, I thought she must be a girl to be that small. My early pregnancy weight was 117, and I was five foot six, so I was not so large myself. But from my experience in nursing school clinicals in the nursery, the babies of that low weight were usually the girl babies. The five-pound range infants were my favorites. They were the cutest. I didn't get to see my cute, little curly-haired baby. To this day, I have never seen her baby pictures.

Pro-life activists will approve of my choosing adoption instead of abortion, and I agree that it was much better than choosing to abort my baby. However, the main dissatisfaction and regret I have is related to the secrecy and closed adoption arrangement I unwittingly agreed to. Various levels of openness, in which birth parents and prospective parents get to know each other on some level, could make it more humane and appealing to pregnant women considering their options.

43

My memory of waking from anesthesia in the middle of the night after giving birth is fairly clear. I have already recounted this experience at the beginning of this memoir. My sense of loss was unexpected. In the next few days, I cried a lot.

Returning to the apartment from the hospital seemed like a lonely event. Diane and the other nurse who shared the apartment were at work. I think the adoptive parents' lawyer dropped me off after the awful signature session in the judge's chambers, but I have only a haunting memory of this. I wasn't scheduled to return to work for several weeks. At the time, it was hospital policy to take a few months off work after delivering a baby.

I hadn't developed much in the way of hobbies or anything by that time in my life, so I felt at a loss for what to do with myself. I recall that I took the two non-uniform maternity outfits I had worn when off duty and threw them away with a feeling of revulsion. One had been a gray color, not my favorite and not flattering. I wasn't yet in the habit of donating to thrift shops, assuming they even existed in those days. Being the frugal person I was, and still am, I kept some of the loose uniform tops. They passed for regular non-maternity wear, and maybe I kept them with high hopes of needing them for a happier pregnancy.

I recall daydreaming that I had kept the baby and taken it to show Josh, perhaps hoping that once he saw our baby he would step up and offer to be a dad. But still, did I want him for a husband?

It seems I made a trip home to Missouri during the weeks I had off after giving birth. I recall holding one of my infant nephews and thinking, "This would have been like holding my own baby." Still, I told no one other than my one sister about my baby, who was now in her new home, enriching the lives of her adoptive family. Ironically, as I learned years later, the sister who knew about my situation lived within about a half hour of my baby's new home in Kansas.

I tried to compartmentalize my grief by stuffing it into a part of my mind that I purposely avoided being conscious of. If doubts came to the surface, I would repeat the mantra, "I did the right thing for myself and the baby." I needed to get on with my life.

# Marriage #1

And so, I got on with my life but with emotional blinders on. I began dating one of the guys, John, who worked in the respiratory therapy department in the hospital where I returned to work. He was going to college and seemed nice enough. I had transferred to the cardiac intensive care unit and saw many respiratory therapists in my work there.

John and I spent a lot of time together and seemed to enjoy the same music, movies and being with mutual friends our age. Things went pretty fast, and soon we discussed getting married. I recall thinking that I would be able to get pregnant and keep the baby after marrying him. I was not head over heels in love but told myself that I loved him enough.

Almost nine months to the day following my giving birth to Rose, John and I got married in a Catholic church in Tulsa with all the usual customs, including a pre-wedding shower, a rehearsal dinner, bridesmaids, ring bearer and flower girl, and a simple wedding reception with a wedding cake and mints and nuts in the church hall. It wasn't extravagant, and my mom chastised me for not providing dinner, at least for the out-of-town guests. That shows how little I had communicated or planned the event with my own parents, who would have, by custom, paid for the latter.

We actually had a fun honeymoon on the Gulf Coast, eating seafood and seeing the ocean. We walked down Bourbon Street in New Orleans and drank hurricane cocktails from souvenir goblets.

But upon returning to our married life and apartment in Tulsa, we didn't have much of a loving marriage. We really hardly knew each other. John knew I had recently had a baby and put it up for adoption.

"I hope that doesn't have anything to do with why you wanted to marry me," he once said. I denied that at the time and never really discussed it with him further.

It had a whole lot to do with it, but of course I didn't admit that to him or to myself.

Getting ready for a wedding and then being married to him kept me from thinking about the most monumental event in my life thus far. I learned that fact over the years and through lots of introspection, interspersed with counseling, self-help books and adoption conferences. Poor guy. He was a nice enough human being, from a really nice family. He deserved better than what he got with me in my emotionally traumatized state.

But I tried, I really did. I did the cooking and cleaning and wrote letters to not only my family but his parents as well. "We wouldn't know what was going on with our son if it weren't for your letters," my mother-in-law said. I'm not sure why we weren't using the telephone in those days, but I was a letter writer from way back, so it seemed like the thing to do.

I continued work at the hospital. John started working at a beer club that had live music shows while he continued to finish his degree. I went to the club from time to time and enjoyed the atmosphere there. Learning a new specialty at the hospital as a cardiac ICU nurse further engaged my mind. If I had any contact with former coworkers from the unit where I'd worked while pregnant, I made up a story that the baby died. In many ways, it had died in my mind, and I had not allowed it to live in my heart.

*I became a bride nine months after placing my baby in an adoptive home.*

# The Forgetting and The Denial

I was busy adjusting to many big changes that gave me ample remedy to avoid thinking about the loss I had just experienced. Not least of these was moving to a large big city, Chicago, from the relative suburban life of Tulsa. Another, of course, was living with my new husband and the adjustments that entailed. Suddenly I was cooking, cleaning, laundering and shopping for two as John and I slipped into the old traditional roles of husband and wife. He sat and read the newspaper for what seemed hours, while I was busy exhausting myself doing the household chores for the two of us.

When I think back about my first marriage, I think about the struggle of a relationship with a guy I didn't know well before marrying him on top of adjusting to life in a big city, plus working at a difficult job as a nurse manager at a hospital.

For the first couple of years in Chicago, I would come home after a tiring day on the job to a high-rise apartment not too far from Lincoln Park. It was in a congested urban area of businesses and other high rises far different from the small town or suburban life I had previously experienced. Later we rented a ground-floor flat in a two-story house in a northwest residential area of the city. This new location required a difficult commute by bus or car.

Fortunately, we had some friends that we did things with who we knew from Tulsa and a few other people from both our workplaces.

We enjoyed the local restaurants and sometimes live music performances on Lincoln Avenue. I would occasionally make it back home to Missouri for family visits, but our lives revolved around work and catching up on sleep, household tasks and socializing on weekends.

Then there was a new job at a hospital where I was in a quasi-managerial position with the title of head nurse in a respiratory therapy department. This was a misnomer, as there was only one other nurse in the department, the department manager, who was my boss. I was in charge of scheduling the three shifts of respiratory therapists and supervising equipment cleaning, sterilization and restocking supplies. I was the supervisor of three African-American cleaning ladies from the south side of Chicago who must have viewed me as the white princess air-head whom they had to tolerate. I had little preparation in navigating the cultural or management aspects of my new job.

I would come home exhausted, only to have to make dinner for my new husband and try to tell myself that maybe things would get better if only I gave it time. I remember thinking early on when I realized this marriage wasn't made in heaven, that I wasn't going to leave it, that divorce just didn't happen in my family.

We didn't plan to have children for a while, and then John dropped the bombshell one day that he didn't see how he could bring children into the world who might inherit the asthma he suffered from. I was puzzled by this, as I never witnessed any breathing issues or even the use of inhalers on his part. Supposedly he had suffered greatly as a child. It's just as well we didn't produce children.

The marriage lasted about four and a half years. During that time I was so busy being unhappy about the immediate reality of my life that I seemed to have little time or inclination to think about having given my baby away. Why would I add such a heavy burden onto the others that crowded my mind and emotions?

If I did let the loss of my baby surface at all, I would not let myself think that I had done anything but make the right decision. To think it was a mistake would have probably thrown me into even greater misery and more than I could handle then.

The issue of infertility did not arise in my first marriage. Although I tried to make a go of the relationship, I was still ill-equipped with good communication skills and frankly had not actually learned much about the man I married prior to entering that union. I am sorry that we married. For me it filled a need at the time that soon turned into an exercise of futility. I don't think we loved each other enough to try harder.

But there was light at the end of this long tunnel of dissatisfaction. His name was Peter.

# Marriage #2 and Infertility

As I write this memoir, I find it difficult to be open and forthcoming about something I am not too proud of during this time. Basically, it's because I had an affair with one of John's coworkers. It started when my husband was out of town on a visit to his family for a week and I had a tennis game scheduled with one of my husband's female coworkers. She canceled due to the heat that week, but Peter, who shared an office with John, substituted. Our affair started that day. As I think I made clear, I was in a loveless marriage, and Peter shared that he was too. I was starving for love and physical connection, which, when it arrived in Peter's willing arms, were overpowering.

An accomplished photographer who dabbled in several visual arts, Peter was good looking and very attentive to me. The fact that he was married, and with a young son did begin to weigh on my conscience. I felt somewhat less sinful because we both professed no love for our spouses and told each other we would be divorcing. Definitely driven by lust and what I was sure was true love, I announced to my husband on his return from his vacation, that I was leaving the marriage that very day. I had accepted an offer from a coworker to move into her place until I found one.

It was crystal clear in my mind that I needed to leave my first marriage anyway, affair or not. I didn't know yet what would become of my new relationship, but I was blinded by anything other than being available wherever my new relationship with Peter took me.

It seemed Peter and I had so much in common. We could talk forever, and just had a rhythm between us that was comfortable and fun. I soon found a studio apartment near work and we continued to see each other when we could while he stayed married. Eventually he left his wife and we moved in together soon after. It seemed like "happily ever after" could be a reality.

After about a year, we moved out of Chicago to Madison, Wisconsin. I remember the first time we visited prior to moving there and how impressed we were by the progressive vibe. Even in the early to mid-seventies a lot of townspeople seemed focused on physical fitness much sooner than the rest of the country.

There was a hiking/biking trail that circled Lake Mendota with a shoreline view from the University of Wisconsin's student union terrace. Peter and I sat watching bikers, sailboats and canoes while sipping a beer from Der Rathskeller and eating deep fried cheese curds. We enjoyed the ambience there and then strolled up nearby State Street. Interesting people went in and out of the numerous shops that led to the state capitol at the top of the hill. Coming back later in winter we were amazed to see sailboats still out on the lake skimming along on the ice but not hitting the numerous fishing shacks that dotted the lake.

We decided Madison was the place for us and found a duplex to rent with a real yard and a nearby pond with red-winged blackbirds within walking distance. It seemed idyllic after my high-rise and two-flat congested living in Chicago.

We were in love and young. I easily got a job in one of the hospitals in town and Peter began his free-lance writing career in earnest. He had done a lot of writing in the past and had published articles previously. He began to earn money as a writer/photographer, and I brought in a regular paycheck to keep the lights on and food on the table. His occasional payments helped, but he was also helping support a young son.

At one point I started to think about getting pregnant, but I wanted to be married. I started broaching the possibility of us getting married, but he wasn't overly enthusiastic. I made occasional comments about returning to Missouri to live closer to my family. He didn't like the sound of that, so he finally agreed that we could get married and stay in Madison. Not having gotten a Catholic sanctioned annulment, we had a private ceremony at a little stone church with only the minister and a couple close friends as witnesses. We honeymooned briefly in the Wisconsin Dells.

Now married, thoughts of finally getting a baby I could keep started to surface. It wasn't until a couple of years passed along with a move to a new house in the country, that it seemed time to populate the nest for sure.

But we ran into some problems with that effort. Although his enthusiasm wasn't as strong as mine to have a child, we had expectations of pregnancy as soon as I stopped taking oral contraceptives. Along with the majority of practicing Catholic couples, we had no scruples about this method of birth control, although it was, and still is, prohibited by the Catholic church.

After about a year of trying to get pregnant, it became an uncomfortable reality that we needed to seek infertility treatment. Peter endured the humiliation of sperm testing, which determined he was somewhat deficient in that area. However, he had conceived one child in the past, so we chalked it up to a batch of semen that had gotten cold and lazy on the way to the clinic after he procured a sample at home.

When I did finally miss a period, we were very optimistic. Then when the pregnancy test was positive, I was ecstatic. It seemed at the time that Peter was too. The nurse in the OB/Gyn doctor's office had me start taking prenatal vitamins. This was evidence to me that I was finally going to have a baby, and I could keep him or her this time. I remember I kept the vitamins out in a prominent spot on our kitchen counter as a kind of frequent testimony of our new status as future parents.

But ominous symptoms arose during the first trimester of the pregnancy. I started to have small amounts of blood appear on my underwear. At my next visit to the doctor, he seemed worried about it and seemed hesitant when I said my baby would be born at about the same time as the baby of a close friend of ours. "They'll be born within weeks of each other," I happily said to the doctor when I told him of my expectations. "Well don't plan too far ahead," he said. "Sometimes it's best not to," he added.

Undaunted, I continued to be hopeful and kept taking the vitamins. This optimism soon ended when I had sudden intractable pain in my side one day. Tests revealed an ectopic pregnancy. The embryo was stuck in one of my fallopian tubes and had not traveled into the uterus to make its home there in a warm inviting lining.

I understood as a nurse that the pregnancy would have to be surgically ended or I would bleed to death. My sisters and my mother expressed sadness and asked "Isn't there some way they could save the baby?" I knew there wasn't, and surgery was soon scheduled.

I was in surgery for several hours and Peter waited in the surgery waiting room. One of my coworkers told me later, "He sure must love you a lot, he was so extremely worried about you when I stopped in the waiting room to find out how you were doing."

The doctor, knowing how much I wanted a baby, spent extra time and effort trying to save my fallopian tube, because he said the other one looked scarred and not able to allow a future embryo to travel through it to the uterus. I thought back to the time shortly after my honeymoon with Peter when I had a case of pelvic inflammatory disease caused by E. Coli, a common bacterium possibly spread from the gastrointestinal tract. This very likely could have caused the scarring in my tubes that resulted in the ectopic pregnancy.

One would think that Peter and I would have been devastated by the ending of my pregnancy, however the fact that we could conceive at all gave us a boost in our optimism about achieving a future pregnancy. But I was sad about losing that baby and had asked the doctor, "What did the baby look like?" I'm not sure I used the word "baby" but I wanted some sort of idea at what stage it was. Were there little hands and feet? Was there anything resembling a tiny human?

I recall his answer was somewhat dismissive and casual. "Oh, it was not recognizable, just a collection of tissues."

My intense need to have a child was, among others, that led to severe cracks in my marriage to Peter. "Sometimes I feel like all you want me for is to make you pregnant," Peter had said. Having sex just at the right time in my ovulation cycle only to become tearful whenever I subsequently started my period was a frequent downer in our relationship. He was busy with his career as a writer and a photographer and wanted to move on.

One day he announced, "I just don't want to try anymore." I looked at him in disbelief, feeling like he'd punched me in the stomach. "I have a kid, and I don't want any more. It's just too hard to keep trying and failing."

At this point, we tried counseling, but it didn't seem to resolve anything. One of the counselors who I met with alone told me that, because of my core need to have a child, I should leave the marriage if he was not going to help me fulfill that important need.

This was hard to accept, and I'm not sure I would have given up on the marriage at that point. However, something occurred during this troubled time in our marriage that crossed my red line.

He periodically went on solo trips to Chicago to visit his son and then stayed and visited his parents. One time I needed to ask him something while he was on such a trip and called his parents' home. When they told me they hadn't seen him, I suspected he was staying with a woman. I had been suspicious that he was having an affair for some time, which was confirmed in my mind. When confronted about this upon his return, he denied having an affair. But I knew he was capable of infidelity. After all, he'd had an affair with me while married to his first wife.

At one point we had even applied for adoption during our marriage. Just as we were breaking up, we got a call from the agency asking if we were still interested and that there might be a baby for us. "No, I'm sorry, but we're no longer interested in adopting," I told them. It became apparent that I would never achieve my dream of having my own children.

Perhaps this spurred me to keep searching for the one that got away. I certainly had the time and other resources to pursue a search, not having my own children to consume my time, and then once separated from Peter, the emotional energy, at least what remained after leaving a marriage to a man I still felt I still loved.

# The Awakening and the Adoption Activist

So, there I was, one fallopian tube down, the remaining one in a post-ectopic pregnancy state of repair. The likelihood of achieving parenthood was pretty unlikely.

It was about this time that my awakening to the loss of my baby Rose became more prominent in my consciousness.

Sometime during my marriage to Peter, I read a magazine article that made me think a lot about my being a birth mother and having a child out there somewhere.

It was a true story of a birth mother's reunion with a son she'd placed for adoption 15 years previously. I don't recall if she contacted his family through the agency or if they tried to contact her. The son was having some problems, and the adoptive family thought getting some answers about his family of origin might help.

As it turned out in the article, the reunion with his birth mother made all the difference in helping this boy to understand the reasons why she didn't think she could keep him. She assured him that she loved him but thought it was best for both of them if he went to a family who could give him a much better life than she could offer at the time of his birth.

I had not entertained the idea that my child, who would have been about 13 at that time, would have a need to know more about why I placed her and possibly to meet me. It was like a big light turned on, and I needed to reach out to her.

I did not know how to contact her family and with no intermediary like a social service agency. I contacted the organization listed in the article, Concerned United Birth Parents, with the acronym CUB.

In the years ahead, I became more and more involved in what is called triad support groups. In the adoption world, the triad refers to the adopted person or adoptee for short, birth parents, generally mothers but many birth fathers also, and last but equal, adoptive parents, many of whom understand the benefits of more openness in adoption. Many adoptive parents fear opening Pandora's box and finding birth parents with unstable, chaotic lives.

Thus began my education and exploration into the adoption triad support community with my membership in CUB, Adoption Information and Direction in Madison, Wisconsin, and the international American Adoption Congress.

I read their newsletters, recommended books, and attended local, regional and national conferences. Most of what I read led me to believe that most adoptees wanted to learn about and eventually meet their families of origin.

Peter did not favor me opening up this long-submerged area of my life. "What's done is done," he said in so many words. He was not on board nor in tune with my new need to finally deal with my grief and learn more from the adoption community.

Undaunted, I found a local triad group in Madison that I eventually joined. Previously I had only been involved for a while with the national birth parent group, CUB.

I devoured books on the subject. There were several that really opened my eyes. One was Dear Birth Parent: Thank You for Our Baby by Kathleen Silber and Phylis Speedlin. When the book was published in the early 80s, Silber was the director of the San Antonio Office of the Lutheran Social Service of Texas. Speedlin was an adoptive parent who founded the Adoption Awareness Center in San Antonio, a training and support agency for those in post-placement adoption lives. The subtitle of their book is "A creative approach to adoption through letters exchanged by adoptive parents and birth parents." I found the real-life letters printed in the book extremely enlightening. They decreased my feeling of isolation as a birth mother. They revealed to me how my decision may have been best, but my daughter's closed, secret adoption was not how I would have done it had I known there were other ways.

The second eye-opener was The Adoption Triangle by Arthur D. Sorosky, M.D, Annette Baran, M.S.W., and Reuben Pannor, M.S.W. This book is considered a classic on how sealed and open records affect the triad. The idea that secrecy was always best between members of the triad was definitely called into question in this book.

Maybe the top of my reading list, and should be for anyone who wants to explore adoption practice, is Lost and Found by Betty Jean Lifton, Ph.D., a psychotherapist and advocate for adoption reform. First published in 1979 in the United States, the book challenges many states' policies of keeping birth records closed. It is a comprehensive discussion of the effects of adoption on all in the adoption triad.

Although many more relevant books have been written since those I mentioned here, these were the main ones, along with my participation in adoption-related support groups, that made me conclude that I needed to deal with this experience. Additionally, it made me question my long-held belief that I had "made the right decision."

The first group I joined, Concerned United Birthparents or CUB, has a logo of a mother bear with her cub. As of this writing, it is still active, with several chapters in some of the large cities in the United States. According to their website https://www.cubirth parents.org/, it is the only organization focused on birth parents.

Although there were no local CUB groups where I lived, I joined and got their newsletter. I read much of the literature they recommended and started to question my decision even more. I read about reunions between birth parents and the children they had placed and wondered if a reunion was something in my future.

In many ways, my reading made me feel like a victim, someone who had been taken advantage of by a society that, at the time of my pregnancy and even decades later, still frowned upon unwed mothers. I realized how my adoption experience mirrored many adoption services that focused mainly on the needs and desires of the adoptive family while erroneously claiming it focused on the best outcome for the baby. My needs as a birth parent were, for the most part, not considered, especially after the adoption. The secrecy surrounding Rose's adoption by people I had never met was not the best way to do it. Other options had been available that I had simply not known about.

As I read more on the subject then and experienced the inability to conceive after trying for over a year, I began to fully grieve the loss of my baby, something I had avoided other than the week of non-stop crying immediately after her birth. I began to think of the chance I had missed to keep Rose had I only had the courage and better information.

For several years I had memberships in both CUB and a local triad group, Adoption Information and Direction (AID), based in Madison.

The AID meetings were well attended, with mainly adoptees and birth mothers but also a sprinkling of adoptive parents. Several of the birth parents were not on the same page as I was in the victim role but were seemingly convinced that their choice to place their babies had been the right one. But they tolerated me, and I learned a lot in the group.

Much of the activity, other than mutual emotional support for post-adoption issues, was searching for birth parents by adoptees or searching for the adoptee by birth parents, again mainly searching for birth mothers.

There were times that birth mothers met as a subgroup, but I preferred the full triad group. It seemed to me that the birth mothers would get into fairly deep and lengthy discussions of how hard it was to go through the placement and sometimes residual grief that erupted at times such as their child's birthdays or holidays. I found the sharing of grief to feel too intense at times. Often it felt like wallowing and reviewing the same hurts repeatedly. I wanted to do something about it beyond grieving.

For a time, I was a state representative for an international organization, the National Adoption Congress (AAC), and fielded, then redirected inquiries about searching in my state. When I decided that searching for my child was something I wanted to do, my local group couldn't help me much because my daughter's adoption had been in Oklahoma; at least, that's what I thought. Later I learned my baby was taken to Kansas, where the adoptive parents lived, and her adoption was finalized. The irony that her family lived in a small Kansas town less than 30 miles from where my sister Margie moved to when Rose was still a toddler has only recently sunk in.

From my reading, adoption conference sessions, and membership in local and national support groups, I gained more and more information about the effects of adoption on the adopted person and others in the triad.

I attended several national conferences sponsored by the AAC, which describes itself as an international organization of regional search, support and advocacy groups. There were many personal testimonies in my home group and in national and regional conferences from adoptees who longed to know their birth families and start a relationship. Although initially hesitant about it, I pursued searching for my lost child with increased resolve.

I was fairly conscious that my continued infertility added to the intensity of my wish to find her. Maybe she needed me, but I needed her too, perhaps the only child I would ever have.

# My Local Support Group

Before going into telling about support groups, I want to introduce one of the main supporters in my life as a birth parent, my husband Glenn, who, in many respects, is the first of my husbands who is truly committed to being married to me and being there for me emotionally. We've passed our 20th anniversary, and as far as I know and desire, we'll continue on our road together until death do us part. Others in my family and friendships have been invaluable, along with counselors from time to time through the years.

That being said, nothing can compare to other people who have gone through whatever struggle or tragedy we endure along our life's journey. As I continued to come to terms with my loss of Rose, I sought out others in the adoption community.

I attended numerous regional and international conferences on adoption, mainly attended by triad members made up of adoptees, birth parents, and adoptive parents, but also many adoption social workers. Before meeting Rose, I started a local group for birth mothers. I had little knowledge of starting a group like this, and my first attempt to meet at a building at my parish church never got off the ground. Eventually, I teamed up with an adoptee, Nancy, and we co-founded a triad group.

We called our group the Adoption Triad Connection (ATC) and met in various locations, such as the local library and church meeting rooms. One of the attendees, Mary Helen, volunteered as a searcher. She had lots of experience finding people in her role as a genealogist at our county's historical society. She had helped a friend who was an adoptee to find her birth family and found it to be an interesting and satisfying pursuit. She became the third member, along with Nancy and me, who stuck with the group until we disbanded ten years later.

*My husband Glenn and I on our wedding day in 1999*

One of the most memorable searches that came out of our triad group was for a birth mother named Elena. She had been madly in love with her high school boyfriend and became pregnant. As a teen with few resources, she placed her baby for adoption and, like many birth mothers, later wanted to find and possibly meet him. Several facets of her search stand out. I don't recall her diagnosis, but she was suffering from an illness that left her fatigued and with such mobility difficulties that she could hardly go up or down stairs when she attended an ATC meeting where we gathered in the lower level of my home.

Our group supported her emotionally and helped locate her son who lived about 150 miles away. During her search, she reconnected with her old boyfriend, her child's father, and they discovered their feelings for each other had not completely died. Getting her son's phone number and address was a bit of a challenge, as it depended on going through his adoptive mother, who wasn't really on board with the reunion idea. I recall having a couple of difficult phone conversations with her and finally getting her to agree to pass on the request for a reunion with Elena to her son, who was now in his forties.

As it turned out, the birth son was indeed interested in meeting her. By then, the birth father was in on the search and was included in meeting plans. However, he wanted to keep his reunion with Elena and his birth son a secret from his current wife and children.

Elena, who was ecstatic to meet her son, was conflicted because she was married, yet seemingly amazed to still have feelings for her high school sweetheart. In a short time, she came to a triad meeting beaming and excited to show us photos of her son and tell us all about the reunion. To my knowledge, Elena never acted upon her feelings toward the birth father by resuming their once loving relationship.

Soon after this, I ran across Elena's obituary in the local paper. There was still time to go to her funeral, so I met her son, his girlfriend, as well as her husband, a few friends and relatives. I introduced myself to her husband and told him how I knew his wife. He treated me like a celebrity and introduced me to the other attendees as one who helped Elena find her son.

I only briefly talked to her son. After our introduction, he didn't seem ready to talk with me further. I thought he seemed a bit shy and somewhat overwhelmed to be amongst his newly found mother's family and at her funeral to boot. Elena's high school sweetheart was not there, as far as I know. I had not previously met him and would not recognize him if he had been.

I recall that Elena had mentioned that her health problems might cause her imminent death. My other triad friends and I felt grateful that we were able to help her find her son and that she had a good reunion with him before she died. Elena had told me that her son and his birth father had visited several times after the initial reunion and seemed to hit it off. I suspect they continued an ongoing relationship, which may have filled a void in the son's life.

Most attendees and people who contacted the ATC were adoptees looking to find their birth parents. There were a few birth mothers from time to time, but few continued as regular group members. Occasionally adoptive parents came, but usually as support to their adopted adult children.

Our group participated in state legislative lobbying efforts, along with others in the triad, from all over the state to ask our legislators to enact a law allowing adoptees to obtain their original, unamended and non-redacted birth certificate. Redacted means nothing is covered up to be unreadable.

Finally, on January 1, 2018, adoptees born in Missouri were granted rights, with restrictions, to their original birth certificates under the Missouri Adoptee Rights Act. See the appendix for more information about this.

# Finally Telling my Family

Before becoming an adoption-reform activist and learning about adoption triad issues, I had not only kept my own brain in the dark as far as dealing with having given a baby away, but I had kept it a secret from most of my family. The one exception was my sister Margie. She was four years older and wasn't married at the time of my pregnancy. I had two other sisters I might have confided in, but they were in various stages of becoming Benedictine nuns in the Catholic Church and seemed too far away and involved in godly matters unconnected to my current situation.

I probably told Margie in a letter, perhaps over the phone. She came to visit me in Tulsa during the latter part of my pregnancy when she could get away from her job in Kansas City. She was supportive in her quiet, nonjudgmental way, and I felt comforted that at least someone in the family knew.

But now that I was searching and learning that secrecy in adoption, as in many other areas of life, is often emotionally harmful, I decided to tell my family.

I started with the easier ones first, which included my niece Kathy. She was six years younger than I was and much like a sister. We shared a lot about our personal lives, visited each other when possible, and had much in common. Ironically, she later suffered infertility and became an adoptive mother of two children whom she and her husband received soon after the babies were born. I will share some of her adoption experience elsewhere in this memoir and one of her daughter's reunion experiences with her birth parents.

I must have told many of my brothers, sisters and other people I was close to by then, and now it was time to bite the bullet and tell my parents. They were both in their early 70s, and dad was enjoying his retirement from his job as postmaster in the small town where I grew up. Mom was, in a sense, enjoying her retirement too from being a mother to eight children and having the main responsibility for cooking, laundering and much of the day-to-day household chores.

They were truly enjoying their golden years. They weren't yet plagued by many aging seniors' myriad health issues. They enjoyed playing cards with friends, church involvement, gardening, family dinners and occasional travel, mostly to see near and distant relatives in the Midwest.

So here I come to possibly shatter their lives with this bombshell during one of my trips home from Wisconsin. In this light, it seems somewhat selfish, but I felt I needed to in the happy event I found Rose.

It was a summer day, as I recall, and I'd made the decision to tell them separately, perhaps not a good choice, but again, true to my avoidant nature, it seemed the easier approach. So I said to my dad one morning, "Would you like to go for a walk?" This wasn't uncommon, as I was a walker and a bicyclist, and my father was always fairly active with gardening, big and small chores around the house and was an occasional bicyclist himself. He readily agreed, and we took off down the street toward the country gravel roads less than a quarter mile away.

We were walking on one of those gravel roads when I managed to get it out as best I could. "Dad, there's something I want to tell you that may be hard for you to hear, but I need to tell you anyway." I believe I had his attention and just said it as quickly as possible. "Right after nursing school, I got pregnant. It was with someone I didn't want to marry, and I put the baby up for adoption. I'm looking for her now, and if I find her, well, I thought it would be good if you and Mom knew about it." I didn't go into why I'd kept it a secret, nor did I elaborate much. I kind of expected some questions from him.

He didn't really react so much that I could tell, but then we walked side by side, not looking into each other's faces. He obviously was absorbing what I had said, and in his stoic German manner, he would not react dramatically. Still, I thought I'd get some sort of reaction, but he said rather quickly and unemotionally, "Well, I'm glad you didn't have an abortion."

Even though abortions on demand weren't legal in 1968 when I got pregnant, they were available to those who sought them. As I previously wrote, I learned from several women I knew that they had had abortions during that period. We continued our walk without discussing it further, that I recall. I think I told him that I would be sharing this with Mom during the remainder of my visit.

Telling Mom was not so easy. Later that day, she was working in the kitchen preparing something for us to eat for supper, I recall. She had her back to me, and I sat at the kitchen table a few feet away. I was sitting near the radio in the corner; that had been the first avenue of knowledge for me that an "unwed mother" had sinned in my mother's eyes.

She must have turned around because I could see her stricken face in my mind even today, right after I told her. I don't recall what I told her, probably much like I told Dad. He was by this time elsewhere in town, in the garden, or puttering in the basement. I do recall telling her that most of the rest of the family knew about it. That was a mistake.

"So, I'm one of the last to know?" she said with what I interpreted as anger. As I write this, I realize it was probably mainly hurt, commingled with betrayal and disappointment. (*Reader, you should know I am crying now as I write this. It's been 37 years.*)

I was somewhat stunned and didn't know what to say. Finally, I asked, "Do you have any questions?"

"What kind of questions should I have?" she blurted out. "Well, I don't know, maybe 'Who was the father?'" I suggested.

She was standing by the stove looking at me after hearing what must have felt like hearing someone had just died that she loved. I told her that it was Josh. He had been to one of the family reunions in the town park we had the year before. Uncle Ray had offered him a beer, I recall. No, she didn't remember him at all.

"Well, what's done is done," she finally said, still with an angry, disappointed tone. It was about then that the doorbell rang. Further disaster.

The daughter of an elderly lady from across the street was at the door making a social call. I don't recall her ever coming to visit before. Why now? Perhaps she was lonely. Her husband had recently died, and she shared some of that experience as my mother, and I sat listening and trying to be cordial. Mom was ringing her hands and fidgety, not her usual composed demeanor. The new widow, probably somewhat mystified by my mother's strange behavior, finally left after what seemed a very long time.

It couldn't have been much worse timing. I had hoped somewhere in the back of my mind to maybe get a bit of sympathy or understanding from my mother about how hard it must have been for me. But this was emblematic of our relationship, I suppose. We didn't deal with emotions too well. We loved each other, to be sure, but we couldn't really share our deepest feelings.

We were of German ancestry, both sides all the way back. Mom's dad was six when he came with his family from the Saxony region on a ship to America. Her mother, too, was from a German immigrant family. Dad's grandparents were from the Alsace Lorraine region, and he was sometimes more emotionally expressive, the French influence perhaps.

We went our separate ways in the house, which wasn't very big. I don't think any of us brought up the subject again during that visit. Each of us handled it in our own way. I assume Mom and Dad discussed it when alone together and processed it as best they could.

One of my sisters told me later that Mom had told her shortly after hearing the awful news from Judy, "I wished she'd never told me."

So there you go. But at least it was out in the open now. I felt a sense of relief that the whole family knew now. I continued with my life, marriage and job, and I kept searching for my lost child.

On one of my subsequent visits home, Mom and Dad had apparently come to some resolution of sorts. They were both eager to show me a little article that had appeared in the local paper. It was a report about a woman from our hometown who had stopped and talked to some people in the area. As a tiny baby, she had been discovered in a mailbox by a rural postal carrier. She had been placed there shortly after birth, but in a spot where someone knew a mail carrier would soon find her.

"I remember when that happened," Dad said. He'd been working in the Post Office then and knew the mail carrier.

The gist of the article was that the woman had gone to a good home and that she had something to tell the people of the area. "I turned out just fine," she was quoted as saying. I think she was saying this to benefit her unknown birth family, who might still be in our small town or its countryside.

I think my parents wanted me to know that it was a happy ending for that adopted person, and that maybe it was the same for my child, the grandchild they didn't know yet. A big message for me was that they were a bit more accepting of the fact that I had had a baby out of wedlock. It happened to other good people too. It could work out okay.

# Adoption Conferences

I attended numerous conferences all over the country with presentations and workshops about topics for adoption professionals and triad members. A typical workshop I attended was one on the subject of birth mothers searching for their children. During the workshop, I voiced my yearning to find out what happened to the baby I had placed. A woman came up to me after the session and spoke to me about how she envied me. "At least you have someone to look for," she said sadly. "I had an abortion, and now I have no one to look for."

I attended several national conferences that lasted several days. I flew to Seattle, San Antonio, Columbus and Kansas City, hoping to gain information about searching and understanding what adoptees, adoptive parents, and other birth mothers experienced. There were a few birth fathers who participated as well. People who had written books on various aspects of adoption had their books for sale in the book room that was always part of these conferences.

Generally, the presentations were informative, sometimes very intense, and they caused me emotional pain on many occasions. Some talks made me angry, such as revelations of adoption abuse at the hands of the notorious Georgia Tann, described by many sources as a child trafficker who operated the Tennessee Children's Home Society in Memphis, Tennessee. She is accused of stealing thousands of children and placing them in adoptive families for profit from the 1920s to 1950. She is not the only supposedly respected member of our American citizenry who profited from adoption services to the affluent at the expense of others less affluent or connected.

There were numerous presentations by adoption professionals, some of whom told about their agency's open adoption practice. This was a new concept to me. My child was adopted in a closed, secretive adoption in which it was understood my being a birth mother would not be divulged to anyone. After all, it was such a shameful thing, wasn't it, even in 1969, during what many referred to as the sexual revolution, to have a baby as an unmarried woman? Later in counseling, one of my counselors told me she understood why I would want to continue keeping it a secret. She explained that many more liberated women of the feminist mindset disapproved of giving away their own babies. So, we were shamed by both the liberal and conservative ends of our society.

But at the conferences, it was refreshing to be among others who understood the world of birth mothers. It was heartening for me to listen to adoptees who wanted to find and have a relationship with their birth families. Many sought only to find the birth mother. Many wanted to know if they had any siblings out there somewhere.

I took lots of notes that I acted on when I got back home. One of my first actions was to send a letter to vital records in Oklahoma to tell them that if my daughter ever tried to find out about me, they had permission to tell her my identity and address.

Another thing I did was write a letter to the doctor who delivered Rose, requesting he contact the adoptive family and give them my contact information in case they or Rose wanted more information from me or wanted to get in touch with me.

# Family Gatherings

My immediate family was large, and we enjoyed each other's company. We would often celebrate holidays, birthdays, and baptisms together at either my parents' home or one of my married brothers' homes. I would attend all I could if my work schedule and the distance from the city I lived in didn't prohibit travel.

When I lived in Madison, Wisconsin, nearby rural Blue Mounds or Chicago, I sometimes couldn't make it because of not getting enough time off or the inconvenience and complicated process of just getting there from such a distance. Bad weather and dangerous traveling also often occurred at Thanksgiving and Christmas.

I longed to attend each gathering as they came up and would suffer a kind of heartache at missing out. I experienced a lot of that when I was in boarding school, and then it happened again as an adult.

While the family gathering was happening, I would often call my parents' home and talk to whoever wanted to take the phone and talk to me for a few minutes. I could hear the chatter and laughter in the background during these calls. Sometimes I felt worse after the phone calls because it accentuated the feeling that I was missing out. I regretted not seeing my parents and siblings, but even more, I hated the fact that I wasn't there to see my nieces and nephews during their growing years.

This discontent was the tradeoff for following whichever man I attached myself to. In addition to missing my family of origin, I had a vague feeling of another loss that became more apparent and real

*Author, top row left, poses with her siblings and parents at a family celebration when her mother was guest of honor, probably her birthday.*

once I began to deal with my being a birth mother. I had given away my child, a child that could have been a part of my life and the lives of my family. She would have had cousins with whom she could have ridden bikes all over the small-town streets of Pilot Grove, and played badminton, hide and seek or the old-fashioned game of croquet in my parents' backyard.

# Marriage #3

After my separation from Peter, I shared a house in Madison, Wisconsin, with another woman, then got my own apartment. I lived a single life for a time after my divorce, but in my conscious thoughts and yearnings, I still wanted marriage and children. Along came a very nice man who seemed very enthusiastic about marrying me. I knew my biological clock was running out of time to get pregnant.

Tom had a lot going for himself and enough love for the both of us, or so it seemed, at the time.

I knew I wasn't in love with him in the Hollywood movie sense, but I thought we could have a good life together. Like me, he was from a large Catholic family; he liked to travel and had a good job, among other characteristics I admired. He was also supportive of my search for Rose.

I knew in my heart that I had not truly gotten over Peter and couldn't wholeheartedly commit. I moved away from Wisconsin back to Missouri to put distance between us and be closer to my family. Tom and I hadn't broken up though and continued to write letters and talk on the phone and got together maybe a couple of times in person. I should have told him no when he asked me to marry him, but I finally said yes to his continuing pursuit. I hoped I was on the path to the family life with Tom I had always dreamed of.

After our small wedding in my hometown church in Pilot Grove we began our married life in a nice home Tom had previously bought in Middleton, Wisconsin, a suburb of Madison.

We soon learned we wouldn't be able to have children. I had a gynecological procedure to improve my chances of conceiving, but it didn't work. I suggested we consider adoption, but Tom did not favor this. We compromised on taking in a Japanese foreign exchange student for her senior year of high school, thinking this would give us a type of parenting, at least for a while.

After about four and a half years, we had serious marital troubles and divorced. I knew for sure I would never have children of my own.

# Letter to a Newspaper

From time to time, I would run across editorials and articles in the paper or other media that would infuriate me with the lack of sensitivity to unwed, vulnerable pregnant girls and women, as well as adoptees and birth parents. Many articles seemed to favor the interests of adoptive parents and rhapsodize about the wonderful institution of adoption.

I wrote a response to an editorial that suggested newborns of teenage girls should be forcibly taken by the state and placed for adoption. My letter appeared in *The Milwaukee Journal* on Sunday, November 28, 1982, in a section called Accent on the News.

**Adoption Choice not That Simple** (*The Milwaukee Journal*'s headline)

*This is in response to the recent "In my opinion" column by Doris Burkart suggesting that "it should be the law that procreators at this age must give up their babies, at birth, for adoption. Children should not be expected or allowed to make momentous decisions affecting another life."*

*I agree that minors should abstain from sexual intercourse for a number of reasons, the most important of which is the risk of conceiving a child before they are emotionally, financially or generally mature enough to be good parents. However, in the society in which we live, it is doubtful that what Burkhart or I think will have any effect on the sexual experimentation of teenagers unless, perhaps, they are our own children.*

*Emotional, financial and maturity factors are extremely important in raising children, but I see many parents 50 years old who are not emotionally, financially or generally mature enough to raise children properly. Should their children be taken from them by the Burkart's of our society, who wish to sit in judgment and separate parents from their children? Should parents be separated forever from their children because they might in the future abuse or neglect them: should they be convicted and sentenced **before** committing the crime?*

*At 21, I conceived a child outside of marriage and did the "mature thing" expected by society in 1969: I gave the baby up for adoption to a couple who could supposedly give her much more than I. I am sorry that I gave my daughter away to strangers. They will never be able to give her the knowledge of her genetic history or tell her that the only thing I lacked at the time of her birth was the confidence and courage to keep her.*

*Present laws governing adoption in most states prevent birth parents like me from ever knowing what happened to the children we gave up. The 2,000 members of Concerned United Birth Parents, a national support group and forum, attest to the fact that our needs have not been met by the adoption system that so willingly took our babies and then turned its back on us, hoping we would forget and not bother them again.*

*I applaud those teenagers who choose not to lose their children to the closed adoption system. I applaud the families who stand behind them and give them the emotional and financial support to keep the child in the family.*

*I am encouraged by agencies such as Catholic Social Services of Green Bay, which handles **only** open adoptions in which the birth*

*parents, adoptive parents and adoptees know each other in a*
*continuing relationship — even after the papers are signed*
*transferring parental rights and responsibilities. This is a healthier*
*and more humane approach than the unthinkable forced surrender of*
*babies suggested by Burkart.*

*Madison, Judy Bock*

I am again amazed that I had the courage (no doubt fueled by outrage) to come out so openly in such a public forum. I was 35 at the time, and it wasn't common knowledge among all my relatives who lived in another state and throughout the Midwest that I was a birth mother. I probably figured that anyone who knew me back home would not be reading the Milwaukee Journal.

# Article Published in a Newspaper

While trying to come to terms with my grief, I reached out to a newspaper columnist whose writing I liked. I admired how he could get to the heart of difficult subjects and have a sympathetic and understanding analysis. My motivation was to educate the public and to share my story with someone I felt I could trust to do a good job of describing my situation. I contacted the columnist, Rob Zaleski, a staff writer for the Madison, Wisconsin, newspaper I subscribed to. Below is his article as it appeared in *The Capital Times* March 12, 1985.

## The Child is Gone, but the Pain Remains

By Rob Zaleski

*It is a balmy Sunday afternoon, one of those rare March days that is perfect for hiking in the Arboretum or strolling down State Street, or the kind of day that might inspire a mother to take her teenage daughter to lunch.*

*Janet, 37, wonders what that would be like. She is peering out the picture window of her suburban home, but her mind is miles away from the robins dancing along the front lawn or the toddlers who are zipping through puddles in their Big Wheels.*

*Sixteen years ago, Janet made what she believes was the biggest mistake of her life. She "surrendered: her daughter for adoption, a decision that haunts her to this day and one that — at least indirectly — may have contributed to the breakup of her first two marriages. I wouldn't talk about the adoption for years," says Janet (not her real name). "It was just too painful.*

*"People tell you that you put the baby up for adoption, and that will be it. But that's not the end. I cried continuously ... I grieved just as someone who grieves a death. However, I didn't get sympathy cards and I couldn't tell my family. So I didn't have any support."*

*Janet, who married for a third time last spring, has decided to go public with her story for several reasons. She feels the media has focused on just one aspect of the adoption process: the joys experienced by the adoptive parents. And she believes that most women who give up a baby for adoption don't comprehend the magnitude of their decision.*

*"They don't realize that the hurting never stops," she says, "and that the older you get, the worse it gets."*

*For Janet, the hurting began in a small town in Missouri in 1968. She had just taken her first full-time job as a registered nurse, when she learned she was pregnant.*

*"Most of my friends were sexually active at that time, like myself, but they were smart enough to be with men they intended to marry," says Janet, who was 21 at the time. Janet says her boyfriend, a college student, not only didn't want to get married, but didn't have the financial resources to help her out.*

*"I remember him telling me that you can't get blood from a turnip," she says. Janet, the youngest of eight kids, says she was too ashamed to tell her parents.*

*For one thing, she says, they are staunch Catholics. For another, "they were pillars of the community."*

*Panic-stricken, Janet says, she packed her bags and headed for Oklahoma, where she moved in with one of her old nursing school friends. The friend helped her through the pregnancy and was in the* delivery room for the birth. She also helped arrange for an "independent" adoption through a local doctor.

Janet, who never saw the baby, says she signed the necessary papers four days after the birth while still on tranquilizers. She says she received no money, although the adoptive parents paid for her hospital expenses.

"I was grieving, but I didn't allow myself to have any second thoughts about what I had done," she says, her voice cracking. "However, I still wonder, if I had seen the child whether I would have been able to let her go. They didn't even tell me her sex."

It wasn't until 12 years later, when she was living in Chicago and her second marriage was foundering, that Janet began toying with the idea of searching for her daughter. Part of the reason, she says, was the startling news that she had fertility problems and probably couldn't have another child. Around the same time, she read a magazine article that told of a woman who — with the assistance of a national group called Concerned United Birth Parents, Inc., which has about 2,000 members — had succeeded in tracking down her child.

"I found out that some adoptees — although certainly not all of them — have an acute need to find out about their birth parents and why they had been given up," says Janet.

Janet says there were two other reasons why she suddenly felt an urgent need to reach her daughter: to give her an update on Janet's family medical history, particularly the news that an aunt had died of breast cancer, and also because "I wanted to make sure she was okay.

Sometimes children aren't actually adopted, they're just sort of floating around in the foster care system."

85

And so the search began, a search that took four years of letters and phone calls, a search against enormous odds and against a system that is heavily weighted in favor of adoptive parents. Last summer, with the help of a private investigator, Janet not only found her daughter, but traveled to the Midwest city in which she lives and viewed her from afar.

"I was very excited, almost like I was in a movie," says Janet. "I've satisfied myself that she seems to be in a very stable family, a family from what I can tell from outward appearances seems to be very family oriented.

"I also was somewhat overwhelmed by the home she lives in ... it was a mansion. I have her address and her phone number, everything that would enable me to make contact. But I'm very concerned about intruding into their privacy ... adoptive parents are very protective, and I'm not sure they would welcome me with open arms."

Janet, her eyes welling with tears, says she probably will wait until her daughter turns 18 before she contacts her and that even then she doesn't expect to form a normal mother-daughter relationship. On the other hand, says Janet, she hopes the adoptive parents realize the young woman has a right to find out who her natural mother is.

"Just because someone doesn't have the resources to parent a child I don't think they should be cut off from her forever," says Janet. "I mean, you're not transferring ownership of a human being. To me, that smacks of the old slave days ..."

If she has just one wish, says Janet, it's that her story might help other young women who may be faced with situations similar to the one she experienced 16 years ago.

*Her advice: "Consider that might be the only child you'll ever have. Also, investigate what is called an open adoption, where a child doesn't lose knowledge of their birth parents.*

*"But most of all ... don't do it. Or be prepared for a lot of grief. Because it doesn't end when you sign a slip of paper. It goes on for the rest of your life."*

One of my birth mother acquaintances from my local triad group gave me some pushback on the last paragraph. She objected to me saying, "don't do it," as she (probably in her 40s at that time) was comfortable with her decision to relinquish her baby to adoption. I don't know if there is adequate data on the number of birth parents that regret their decision versus the ones who don't. During my time as an active member of Concerned United Birthparents, it seemed that the number of those who voiced regrets for choosing to relinquish was predominant.

However, they perhaps were the ones I paid more attention to, I will admit.

# Reconnecting with the Birth Father

Early in my search for Rose, I thought it would be a good idea to contact Josh and let him know that I was searching for our daughter. It had been decades since we had any contact. In fact, I don't think I had ever told him I had given birth. As it turned out, he had the impression I had an abortion. He had inferred this from my request that he help me financially. I know I had never spoken of abortion with him, only that I could use his help financially because I would be taking a leave of absence from my job for several months before and after Rose's birth.

When I met with Josh at a restaurant in the town where he lived in southern Missouri, he confirmed that he thought I'd had an abortion, and that was why I had asked him for money. So it was news to him that he had a daughter out there somewhere. He proceeded to tell me while eating his breakfast that he had also fathered a son with a woman he had dated for a short time after he conceived Rose with me. Years previously, she had brought the child to show him when the boy was just a toddler.

"He was a cute little guy," Josh reminisced in his casual and upbeat manner. I got the impression that he did not have continuing contact with the boy or his mother after their brief meeting. As I learned in subsequent conversations with Josh, and after I had found Rose, he went to considerable trouble to locate the boy's mother.

"I told her to 'sit down once I got her on the phone," Josh told me. "When I told her who I was, she was pretty excited and told me that her son had just been asking her about his father." He was about 12 at the time, Josh said. They arranged a meeting, and he and his son had an instant rapport. They continued to spend time together and developed a fond father-son relationship.

I am unsure if my contacting Josh and meeting him at the restaurant sparked his desire to find the boy he had met as a toddler, but I suspect it might have.

At the restaurant at our first meeting, I half-jokingly suggested, "Maybe we can have a reunion someday with our daughter and your son." They may have met, though not knowing they are half-brother and sister. Josh told me that his son owned and managed a business in a city very near to where Rose lived. Small world.

Because they lived so close to each other and both had children, possibly about the same age, I began to be a little concerned that the children might end up dating each other, not knowing their close blood ties. In one of my letters to Rose, I told her of this concern and the name and business of her half-brother.

In the adoption world, it is uncanny how many birth family members live in close proximity to their unknown relatives who are adopted. This has been reported often at conferences and by news outlets. In Rose's case, she lived as a newborn and possibly into her toddler years in Eudora, Kansas, only 22 miles from where my sister Margie lived near McLouth, Kansas when she married in 1972. Rose would have been about three and a half years old when her biological aunt moved there. I don't know how old Rose was when her family left Eudora, but it's remotely possible their paths crossed somewhere in eastern Kansas.

One story I recall hearing about through the news and reported widely was about a reunion of a birth mother and the son she had placed for adoption, Christine Tallady and Steve Flaig. They were coworkers at a Grand Rapids, Michigan, Lowes store for eight months and had joked around together during their workday as a head cashier and delivery worker, respectively.

Search YouTube if you want to watch a video of their reunion story and many similar close encounter stories.

My concerns about my daughter and her half-sibling were not irrational. After meeting with Josh in the restaurant, I wrote a letter to him.

*April 5, 1983*

*Dear Josh,*

*Thanks for taking time out to meet with me a couple of weeks ago. I'm wondering if you've met your son yet and how that's going for you.*

*I checked one of the search books and it does say to establish paternity to contact the D.A. in the city of birth. Before we do that though, I'd like to write to the court in Tulsa Co. and to the State of Oklahoma Dept. of Human Services Division of Child Welfare to see if they will examine the records and tell me if you are listed as the father. (I vaguely recall telling someone his name for a form they were filling out during my postpartum stay in the hospital. My assumption is that it was for the birth record.)*

*As I think I mentioned to you federal laws do provide certain special rights for Native American adoptees. Specifically U.S. Public Law 95-608, Title III—Recordkeeping, Information Availability, and Timetables clearly states that adoption decrees shall show tribal affiliation and name of tribe of the adopted child. Section 107, title I, of this same law declares, "any Indian who has reached age 18 who was the subject of an adoptive placement, (is entitled) to find out his or her tribal affiliation and any other information that might be necessary to protect any rights from that affiliation." U.S. Public Law*

*95-608, Title III, Section 301 (a), "requires the State court to provide the Secretary (of the Interior) with a copy of the final decree or order of adoption of an Indian child plus information about the tribal affiliation of the child, the names and addresses of the biological parents and adoptive parents, and the identity of any agency having files or information relating to the adoptive placement. This information is not to be subject to the Freedom of Information Act." So I am really very interested to know the specifics regarding your Indian ancestry through your mother. It might be useful someday in providing our daughter, xxxx xxxx xxxxx, with some interesting facts. Diane S. is only 1/32 Indian and has a card that would provide free medical care.*

*Actually breaking and entering would be a lot simpler, but I'm too law abiding for that and will pursue this rather cumbersome legal route. I'd sure like to beat the bureaucrats at their silly game.*

*Rose will be 14 on April 7. When is her brother's birthday? My half joke about a family reunion might not be such a bad idea. A little weird maybe, but it might be good for the kids to meet each other. Anyway that's at least four years in the future if at all.*

*Someday I'm coming back to southern Mo. and it's going to be warm and sunny and I'm going to plop myself down in front of a lake with a fishing pole in one hand and a glass of very good wine in the other. That last trip was not what I had hoped for weather wise. Diane is organizing a 15-year class reunion in August but I don't know if I can make it.*

*Please tell Connie if you see her that I'll try to catch her next time I'm down there.*

*We were in a hurry to leave and I felt rotten with my cold.*

*So if you would, Josh, find out about your mother's tribal affiliation and any documentation to verify it. I'll let you know what I hear about paternity documentation.*

*Your one-time lover and hopefully current friend,*

*Judy Bock*

My thinking on delving into Rose's Indian ancestry on her birth father's side seems very convoluted to me now. I state in the letter to Josh that I want this information to be able to someday tell our daughter about it. This, however, would not require any involvement with the courts and delving into laws pertaining to Indian adoption.

We could just tell her about her ancestry. I think my ultimate goal wasn't well thought out, but maybe I thought Indian adoption law would somehow help me find her. I certainly didn't make it clear in the letter to Josh that my intention in using Indian adoption law was to help in the search.

This effort to make some sort of claim to American Indian ancestry that would somehow help facilitate a reunion was grasping at straws and probably too far out there in reality. At the time, I was not letting any stone unturned. The fact that Rose's potential Indian ancestry through her birth father was not declared at the time of her birth probably made it unlikely that anything could be accomplished through Indian law in eventually finding her.

Another note in my files relating to Josh's suggestion of breaking and entering the lawyer's office probably had no serious intent, but offered the possibility of breaking into the lawyer's office and getting into the files to find information about our daughter's adoption. He seemed serious about it during our March face-to-face conversation just prior to this letter, but maybe this was just blusterous talk on his part that he had no intention of pursuing.

In any event, Josh nor I followed up on delving into Rose's Native American ancestry or breaking and entering. I didn't pursue establishing his paternity on the birth certificate either. It was just too far-fetched and complicated.

Josh and I eventually became Facebook friends, and at first, we talked a little on the phone. There was never any hint on either side of wanting to renew any sort of romantic relationship. We both had committed marriages, and the conversations were mostly limited to the subject of our daughter and meeting her, sometimes about our work and families.

I delayed telling Josh I found Rose until about a year later. He didn't seem upset that I hadn't told him immediately and shared more information about his children and the son from a brief relationship. I delayed telling him because I was concerned that he would try to meet Rose before I had and would mess things up. Years later, after I told him she'd declined to meet me, he talked about going to her home, knocking on her front door and announcing that he was her long-lost dad. I was glad to hear from him a little while later that his wife and daughter dissuaded him from doing that.

I learned through Facebook that he was immersed in his community, his job and his family. He was proud of his family, a classic vintage car, and apparently had plenty of friends. He didn't seem to share a strong need to meet Rose. We eventually lost touch.

# The Adoptive Parents

As I said before, I was not told much, nor did I ask, about the people who would ultimately parent my daughter. The doctor told me that the woman who I thought he was referring to as the likely adoptive mother looked very much like me. In fact, she could have been my sister, he said. I may have seen her face in family photos on Facebook many years later, but I could not be certain it was her.

Rose chuckled a bit at our brief reunion when I told her what the doctor had said. "You don't look anything alike, and she's rather petite," Rose said. If it was her, the woman in the Facebook photo was maybe five feet tall, maybe less. She looked like she had a fair complexion and a pleasant disposition. When Dr. Maddox saw me, I was five foot six, and my hair was brown. I usually had a nice tan.

Perhaps Dr. Maddox was talking about a couple who ultimately didn't adopt Rose, or perhaps he just told me what he wanted me to believe to make me think my child would fit in physically with the family she would be going to.

I believe I saw a photo of Rose's father on LinkedIn. He was a nice-looking, pleasant-looking man in a suit, at the end of middle age, with a full head of hair. The latter attribute was dissimilar to Rose's birth father, who lost a good amount of cranial hair in his later years. I understand that the adoptive father worked in the oil industry in some way, a big leap from his start as a school athletic coach in a small town in Kansas.

Again, I regret I never met them. Back then, at the time of my desperation and decision to relinquish, open adoptions were not unheard of, but probably not that common in Oklahoma and many other states at the time. Many agencies gave the birth mother and father, if the latter was involved, a written description and social profile of potential adoptive couples. Such things as physical descriptions, education, hobbies, jobs, health issues, religion and other information were included. It became common practice by adoption agencies to give a pregnant woman considering an adoption plan several folders of adoptive parents' profiles from which to make this important choice for their child.

Choosing my child's parents from files such as these, even if I never met them in person, would have given me such a feeling of comfort that I had placed my child with the family I thought best for her rather than giving that power over to the doctor. For all I know, he may have picked whatever prospective adoptive couple most recently came to his office or that a mutual friend of his had referred.

Despite this, I can't say I ever felt as though I abandoned my child. I went to a trusted doctor recommended by a dear friend who had lived in Tulsa for many years and knew the doctor by reputation as someone who placed babies with very good families.

# Educating Myself About the Adoption Triad

I attended quite a number of regional and national conferences on adoption triad issues. I was interested to learn of other birth mothers' experiences and how they handled the emotional aftermath of losing a child this way. Another topic of great interest was the effect of adoption on the child. Often there were presentations of reunion experiences, mostly positive, but some with some unexpected negative consequences, that were also shared.

I bought books in the bookstore section of conferences. One that I particularly found useful was <u>How it Feels to be Adopted</u>, by Jill Krementz, true-life accounts of 19 adoptees who share their feelings about being adopted, both good and bad. I continued to read articles and books about adoption from a birth parent's perspective and adoption's effects on adoptees, adoptive parents' perspectives, and a good amount of material on search and reunions.

In more recent years, I gained solace from <u>The Girls Who Went Away</u> by Ann Fessler, who captured some of my experience as a self-banished birth mother. The book is a compilation of interviews with many women who placed their children for adoption in the decades before Roe v. Wade, as the subtitle says.

At conferences, I took notes, some of which survived in my notebook.

Here are a few that give tips on contact:

*Making Contact—Confidential Intermediaries in Washington State at the instruction of court*

*Have letters and pictures from the searcher. Be able to sit down, have quiet time, and do lots of writing while on phone*

*Mock call role-plays of phone call contact.*

*Main things — let the found person know you care, and confidentiality will be maintained. First, verify who it is.*

*Direct contact, discretion is extremely important, deal with the shock*

*Have an address and phone number — say in the first three minutes of conversation, get tuned into your own feelings, avoid any hostility in contact*

*Chuck (probably audience member) — actual contact, call when most likely to be alone. Offer to be in the house at the time of contact*

*I will try to respect your wishes*


My rather sketchy notes from workshops and contacts at the American Adoption Congress conference in Seattle in May '84:

*A phone call is the first choice for initial contact rather than a letter or direct contact. If the first call is a rejection, the next step is a card with a nice picture and grandchild.*

*\*check with Pam* (my note to myself to contact my lawyer) *re: getting copies of the papers I signed from District Court. Also, for her to send a pic.* (I don't think I followed through with this.)

*If a man is a caller, a phone call should be identified as long distance from a place of business and identify the speaker so as not to be misinterpreted as an obscene phone call.*

(These suggestions for contact strategies must have been directed at adoptees contacting birth parents.)

In my notes is the name, address and phone of a person I met who helped locate people separated by adoption. I have the instructions to "*call re: searcher*" by this and to "*start a scrapbook for Jody.*"

# Found at Last

As a result of being persistent in my search and meeting the pivotal person willing to help me, I was put in touch with someone who searched for a fee. It was a mystery as to who the searcher was, and I never learned his/her name.

For a rather hefty fee, I had the name and address of my daughter and her parents within a matter of weeks from the time the search began. It was a matter of trust with the contact I'd made at the conference that an adoption scam artist wasn't taking my money.

I remember getting the phone call on the landline phone, which was the only type of phone at the time. I was in the kitchen when I got the call, and the searcher told me to get a piece of paper and something to write with because she had information about my daughter.

It was July 31, 1984, when Rose was 15. My notes are in pencil on three-hole notebook paper. The searcher told me her adoptive name and where she currently lived. I learned her adoption was finalized in Douglas County, Kansas, a half hour drive from where my sister Margie lived, not in Tulsa as I had assumed. At the time, I was somewhat in shock as I took notes and didn't connect the dots about her adoption being in Kansas and her possibly living so close to my sister.

The surrender document had been notarized by Judge Whit Mauzy on April 11, four days after birth, and my daughter went to her adoptive home on April 15. I don't know who had custody of Rose prior to that. Perhaps she stayed in the nursery at the hospital or perhaps she was with some other person. Rose mentioned something during our eventual reunion meeting that she had been told that as a tiny baby, she was in the lawyer's office waiting for her parents to pick her up.

My notes are incomplete regarding a letter from L.E. Rader of the Oklahoma Department of social services about the transfer of custody, apparently from one state to another.

The searcher told me Rose's adoptive parents' names, where they grew up and their occupations. I learned they were Christian and when and where they married. I was given their address at the time of her adoption and what church they went to, the St. Paul Church of Christ.

How all this information was obtained, I have no idea. In addition, I learned the birth name of Rose's adoptive brother and his birth mother's name as well.

Finally, I got the current address for Rose and her family. It was an affluent suburb of Oklahoma City. Her dad was now employed in the oil business.

Apparently, I registered little emotion over the land line and the searcher voiced surprise that I didn't sound more excited. I suspect there was some shock and resultant numbness on my part, like when you get stunning news of some major event in the family that you can't quite digest in one big gulp.

I have no memory of what I did the rest of the day after I hung up from this earth-shattering call. Did I celebrate? Did I call Diane, my friend who had been with me through the last months of my pregnancy and in the delivery room with me?

I know I did a bit more detective work on my own and learned the office number of Rose's adoptive father and amazingly to me, the "children's telephone" number from the white pages of her hometown phone book. Perhaps I found it through my library. or directory assistance. I don't think the internet was searchable yet for phone numbers like this.

I had no impulse to call any of the numbers nor to hop in the car and go to any of the addresses I had been given. My next moves awaited verification of the information I had been given. I had more detective work and decisions to make.

# Verification and a Visit

Not knowing the searcher and being the skeptic that I am, I felt the need to make sure the information I was given was accurate. After I learned the names and address of my child's family, I set out to find out what I could about them.

I was able to get a copy of Rose Diane's amended birth certificate from the Oklahoma Department of Health vital statistics. It was a non-certified copy for which I paid $15. I vaguely recall that I said in my request that I was a relative doing a family tree and needed the certificate for that purpose.

It was useful in confirming to me that the searcher had found the right person. There were many reports at adoption conferences that, along with the adoptive parents being listed as the parents on amended birth certificates, other data was changed as well. But on her amended certificate, the date and time of birth matched what my hospital record I had previously obtained said about Baby Girl Bock. The birth weights were the same as well. Not a lot of babies were born in the five-pound range, so I thought this was definitely the right person, my daughter. Of course, she was no longer my daughter legally. Someone else had all the rights of parentage to her now.

I was not at all sure what I would do regarding contacting Rose or her family now that I had found her. She was still under the age of 18. Perhaps, like the child I read about in a magazine who had been having a lot of problems, she could benefit from meeting me.

I found her hometown's yellow pages in my local public library and ordered the 1984 and 1985 yearbooks for her town's public schools. I didn't find her there.

In October of 1984, the fall after hearing from the searcher, I visited her hometown with Bruce, my friend Diane's husband, back in Tulsa. As a reminder, Diane was the friend I first confided in that I was pregnant and who suggested the possibility of placing my baby with a couple through Dr. Maddox. Bruce, who was Diane's fiancé at the time, had wheeled me into the hospital the day I went into labor and was assumed by hospital staff to be the father.

I was still in close contact with Bruce and Diane via letters, occasional visits to Tulsa and phone calls. Once I got my daughter's location, it somehow transpired that Bruce and I would go to the town where she lived and find out what we could. We set out on October 19, 1984, for the city where the searcher said she lived. Rose would have been 15 years old at that time.

I had no idea the trip would be so fruitful. I looked at my daughter from a distance, as Bruce met her and her family in their driveway. I chose to stay in the car when we went to their neighborhood because I thought perhaps they would see a definite similarity between Rose and me. Bruce and I were, in a sense, stalking, I suppose, but it was a one-time occurrence to determine if Rose was healthy and happy. It was deceptive but with honorable intentions.

We were lucky to have a chance to encounter her family outside their home. That day was Homecoming parade day for my daughter's school. Just as we approached their address, a van with people in it drove into their driveway and got out. I will always be grateful to Bruce, may he rest in peace, for having the gumption to walk up the driveway before they went into the mansion it was attached to and to initiate a conversation with them.

Our story was that we were checking out the neighborhood as to whether it would be good to purchase a home there. Bruce had a fairly long conversation with my daughter's parents while I was in his car's passenger seat, straining my neck to get a glimpse of them. I could see a family of four exiting the van. It included a man and woman, a young girl in her teens and a younger child.

It was a very long driveway, and Bruce had parked the car on the street. We were probably the equivalent of a football field away. The next day my neck was sore due to the muscle strain of turning my head from my forward-facing position in the passenger seat to see Rose and her family. Bruce returned to the car and told me my daughter was beautiful, as was her mother. "They seem like real nice people," he said matter-of-factly.

Upon his return to the car, his assessment assured me that she was being parented, if appearances and demeanor counted for anything, by upstanding people who were getting on well in the world and could be kind enough to a stranger to give him helpful advice.

Although I didn't get to see my daughter's face up close in person that day, I was able to see it in a photo which we luckily obtained at the school she attended later that day.

My memory fails me of how we decided to visit a small private Christian school in her city. Bruce and I asked at the office for a yearbook and said we were checking out schools for our daughter. We were cordially invited into one of the administrator's offices and given a brief summary of the school's features and programs. He handed us a yearbook and said he hoped we would consider it a good option for our daughter. We said our goodbyes and thanked him and returned to the car in the parking lot.

Still not knowing if this was the school Rose attended, I vividly recall balancing the yearbook on Bruce's car and going through the pages to the grade she should have been in. I read the lists of names on the photo page and visually scrolled to her name, which was actually there. My eyes moved over to the frame on the page where her photo should be. Without counting, I instantly spotted her by recognizing her facial features, eyes, hair, and even her expression, and felt the amazing reality of seeing her face, a face that looked a lot like mine.

"Bruce!" I exclaimed. "Here she is!"

We looked through other pages and found her in numerous clubs. Everything I deduced from her photos and activities indicated a happy, healthy, normal child. That was good, but it indicated that she didn't need me at all, I realized. She was being parented quite well without my interruption in her life now.

But I had found her. It was really her. She was alive and well. By my standards, she was privileged and in an apparently close family who did things together, having gone to the Homecoming activity together as they had told Bruce.

It would be a couple of years until I made actual contact. In the meantime, I subscribed to her local paper and ordered the next yearbook at the end of the school year.

Her hometown newspaper that I started a subscription proved to be useful also, at least the sports pages. To my delight, I found her photos showing her in action on the tennis court. She apparently excelled in the sport, having reached the finals in state competitions and in the number two position for her school, a public high school she then attended.

One of the photos shows her intense focus while reaching for a ball with an extended forehand. Her outstretched body displayed long, sculpted legs and arms. The expression on her face reminded me of my father's when he was concentrating hard. The eyes were focused on the ball with a slight frown, and her tongue appeared slightly visible between determined closed lips. Another trait she probably carried from me was a head of dark, curly and somewhat unruly hair if not controlled by conditioning products or other hair-smoothing methods.

Through Rose's school years, I was able to obtain more yearbooks. I would call the school office and request the address to send my payment. At one school, I said the misleading but true statement that my daughter attended school during such and such year, and I wanted to get a yearbook from that year.

It was gratifying to see all the activities she participated in and additionally to see her image in group photos. Like me, she was on the junior high basketball team and in the Honor Society. She dressed in plaid in many of the photos, which I often wore in my youth. She wore her hair long, unlike me at that age, but she did have bangs as I did and still do. As evidenced in her local paper, she excelled in tennis, and I saw another photo of her with the tennis team in the school yearbook. There were miscellaneous pictures of her I discovered, like the one at what appears to be a lunch counter with possible friends beside her. Scrutinizing her friends' faces and general appearance, I thought she had chosen well if they were regular chums.

As the years rolled by and I looked at her image in subsequent yearbook photos, I got a sense of how she was physically changing and maturing. She was in Key Club, a service and leadership training club in high school and again in the Honor Society. In addition to her sports activities, these extracurricular club memberships told me that she was aspiring to serve others and improve herself, both of which I admired. Not surprisingly, she was a member of the Fellowship of Christian Athletes.

In August of 1986, I took out an ad in the classifieds of her hometown paper, hoping to snag her potential interest in finding her birth family. It read, "ADOPTED? Seeking birth family? Free registry. Send S.A.S.E. to I.S.R.R., P.O. Box 2312 Carson City, Nevada, 89702."

I had registered my information with the International Soundex Reunion Registry (I.S.R.R.) seeking a reunion with Rose should she also contact the registry. It was a well-respected and productive registry known widely in adoption triad organizations. The small cryptic ad probably escaped notice from Rose. I suspect she never looked at the classifieds, wasn't interested in finding her birth family, or she didn't trust whatever the mysterious I.S.R.R. was. It would have taken a very determined teen to follow up on such an ad. Furthermore, although the acronym S.A.S.E. which stood for self-addressed, stamped envelope, was commonly used in the business and literary world of that time, a high school student might not be too familiar with it.

As I later learned, Rose was a very dutiful, respectful child who probably would not have pursued looking for me without her parent's knowledge and consent.

# Professional Grief Counseling

Because Rose was only 15 when I found her and didn't seem to be needing me, I decided not to contact her or her parents yet, even though part of me thought it might be beneficial in case Rose had any identity formation issues resulting in emotional or behavior problems.

Therefore, I just continued getting her hometown newspaper, hoping to see something about her or her family and ordering yearbooks from the school I thought she was attending. This was before the days of Facebook, so public information was limited.

Today I can get on Facebook and see photos of my daughter and her children and learn a little about the highlights of their lives.

Occasionally I would look at Rose's or some of her two older children's Facebook pages. I was able to view photos of special events that were posted publicly or on their profile pages. I downloaded and took some for printing at a drugstore photo department. Rose posted her and Richard's wedding photos on their 25th anniversary, which I had printed and framed. They were a lovely couple who looked so happy. I thought that Rose was especially beautiful that day, even more so than many brides.

Many photos of her oldest daughter that I saw on Facebook were of her numerous formal events. She wore beautiful gowns and was generally part of a group of young, well-dressed and groomed friends. All of them were tattoo-free and without obvious piercings, something I found refreshing in contrast to many youths of that time and today. Frankly, they all looked like they could have been Hallmark movie channel actors and actresses by their outward appearance.

Baseball was a big factor in Rose's son's life. His joy and enthusiasm for the game apparently matched his success on the field as a player. There were many photos of family members posing with him when he was in his baseball uniform.

I would not look at their Facebook pages on a regular basis, but when some inner need drew me. I suspect some would consider me a snoop or stalker. But it was available publicly, and I took the opportunity to learn about the events of their lives without asking to friend any of them or to comment on any of the postings. Without fail, their public posts confirmed my previous conclusion that Rose had a rather wonderful, stable life, full of family, apparent financial security and worthwhile activities.

But I am getting ahead of my story here.

Even though I had found Rose, I continued to go to national conferences and meetings of triad groups. Sometimes I just told my story to newcomers as we went around the circle in whatever group I was sharing my birth parent experience. I know I asked for others' input on whether or not to contact, how to contact, who to contact, whether or not to use an intermediary and so forth.

I periodically availed myself of the opportunity and luxury of personal, professional counseling on the issue. One of my counselors while I lived in Wisconsin, who was himself an adoptive father, and very knowledgeable in triad issues, offered to be an intermediary and facilitate communication between Rose and me and her family. Although I trusted him, I was still cautious and did not take him up on his generous offer. I have had second thoughts about my decision not to accept his help. What if. Perhaps there would have been a different and better outcome than the one that ultimately developed.

Another counselor I stuck with for years was also an adoptive father. Hank encouraged me to write myself a letter about my decision to place my baby in an adoptive home. I was expressing a lot of guilt, grief and regret for doing so. I was able to really look at myself more generously by doing this exercise. I think it helped me forgive myself and sympathize with the young woman I had been.

Here is the letter:

*June 28, 2000*

*Dear Judy,*

*I've been asked to write you a letter of support and understanding. I know what I am supposed to say, but a part of me wants to say, "You stupid girl!" But that sure isn't supportive or understanding, so here goes.*

*I could say how you were, in many ways, a child. You were inexperienced about much of life. You had never been taught to handle any big problems. You'd always been shielded from them, protected by the very people you hid your pregnancy from. You learned how to protect them, perhaps.*

*You hadn't yet learned to talk with someone and consider all your options. You were really scared and mostly ashamed.*

*How could you expect to suddenly have the courage to be open to parents you'd never had an adult conversation with? You had never confided anything to them; how could you expect to easily tell them that you had had sex outside of marriage and now were pregnant? Get real, girl.*

*How sad for you to have been in that situation with no one in your family you really felt at the time you could open up to. Why was that:*

110

*Jim and Dorothy probably would have been understanding and supportive too. For some reason, the idea of talking to them just didn't enter your mind. They were so busy with their kids. My brother Jim and his wife Dorothy lived in the same area as I did when I became pregnant. I was a frequent visitor at their lively home, where they were raising seven children. They were loyal Catholics but likely would not have been judgmental toward me in my situation. In my late pregnancy, I did tell my sister Margie of my pregnancy and plan for adoption. She came to visit me prior to delivery, but we didn't discuss alternatives to my plan. Years later, she expressed regret that she didn't know how to help me then but wished she could have done something more. I told her I was just comforted by her nonjudgmental presence.*

*You had never been one to sit and chat about life's big issues with anyone except your close friends. And that is whom you went to. No mystery here about your actions. Why would you suddenly change your behavior out of the blue and about something so monumental?*

*After all, Diane suggested something that sounded pretty reasonable. You didn't want to marry Josh. You didn't love him. That wasn't such a bad decision. How were you supposed to predict that you would have married two men later that you weren't "in love" with? Don't berate yourself for making that decision about marriage even if it meant not having a father for your baby.*

*I've heard that your daughter had a pretty good childhood and got into what by all indications is a pretty good family. Certainly she got to go to a great school. You know her parents love her by what you can glean from the letter. She lived in a mansion. You saw it with your own eyes. She was well provided for.*

*You will always have some sadness and "what-ifs" related to this. Always. Many people have regrets. You are not alone in your sorrow.*

*Now you have a chance to be a mother. Take it. Go to the ballgame. Be part of Melissa's life. She probably needs you. You need her. Let yourself heal. You can do it. Just do it. It is OK, Judy.*

*The adult you have finally become forgives you.*

*God blesses you Judy. You have been carrying a lot for a long time. It's time to move on, Maybe someday Rose will want to know you. Maybe she does now, but is protecting her parents. Ironic, but probably true.*

*Let's look ahead to the future and the now. It's vacation time and Melissa wants to go on the water slide. Show her and Glenn the Rocky Mountains. The rest of your life is beginning now.*

*With love and understanding, Judith*

*P.S. I should mention that there is a lot of relevance to the fact that two of your sisters were nuns and your situation of wanting to shield your behavior from your family.*


Another of Hank's counseling assignments was to identify losses related to being Rose's birth mother. I identified quite a few.

*August 7, 2000*

1. *Missed cuddling my baby, touching and kissing her toes, looking into her eyes, coaxing her smiles and giggles, and making blowing noises on her tummy.*

2. *Missed seeing her grow and change through the years and picking up Bock family traits.*

3. *Missed seeing who she looks like — how she will carry my genes long after I'm gone.*

4. *I didn't get to know her, talk to her, or find out what she was — her personality, dreams, and talents.*

5. *I didn't get to play tennis with her, go shopping together, go garage sailing, or go out to lunch.*

6. *I lost any love she might have had for me as an infant, small child, and later as an adult.*

7. *I lost the chance to pass on my family values, things my mother taught me, my recycling and environmental values, my love for gardening and my love of flowers.*

8. *I lost the possibility of having her companionship in my mid-life and old age.*

9. *I missed feeling proud when she accomplished something.*

10. *I missed her presence at family gatherings where most of my brothers and sisters had their children.*

11. *My father never got to meet her — something he'd hoped for. My mother will probably not meet her either.*

12. *I missed going out to lunch with my daughter.*

13. *I missed seeing her dressed up for the prom.*

14. *I missed her graduation.*

15. *I will miss knowing her children, my biological grandchildren; I would have loved them.*

16. *I missed passing on family traditions.*

*17. I missed fixing her hair and buying her clothes and presents.*

*18. I lost some self-respect.*

*19. I lost time and money when I took time off at the end of the pregnancy.*

*20. I lost nearness to my family when I left Kansas City to hide in Tulsa, and then from there followed the man I married there to Chicago.*

*21. I lost the chance to have a normal, stable marriage and probably a child/children of my own had I not gotten pregnant when I did.*

*22. I lost the dream I'd always had of a happy marriage and children of my own with the man I loved.*

I repeated myself a number of times with my identification of losses. It seems passing on my and my family's traits were important to me. One of my dreams of having a happy marriage and children with the man I loved finally came true in my current marriage. Although the children and grandchildren are not descended from me biologically, they are my children and grandchildren. The grandkids address me as grandma, and often the kids call me mom, which occurs more noticeably in later years.

September 5, 2000

Another of my counselor's assignments was to identify the resources I had to help with my grief work. The following is what I wrote.

*1. My knowledge of grief after working as a psych nurse for over 12 years and having attended grief workshops, much reading on the subject and reporting and writing a lengthy article on the grief work of a family who lost a child in a tragic accident*

2. *A supportive husband who is active in Joyful Again, a Catholic workshop program for grieving widows and widowers*

3. *Supportive friends at work (Boone), family members, and my counselor*

4. *Spiritual resources*

5. *Patience and persistence*

6. *Here is a list of people who I believe will be supportive:*

*My brothers and sisters, my niece Kathy and her husband Rick, Martie, Barbara H., my mother, the American Adoption Congress, Diane and Bruce, nursing school chums, Edra, Susie, Our Lady of Peace nuns, Hank, Glenn*

Another assignment: Things to continue to work on resolving from my loss list:

I identified number one: "cuddling my baby, touching and kissing her toes, looking into her eyes, coaxing her smiles and giggles, and making blowing noises on her tummy," number 8: "I lost the possibility of having her companionship in my mid-life and old age," number 21: "I lost the chance to have a normal, stable marriage and probably a child/children of my own had I not gotten pregnant when I did" and finally number 22: "I lost the dream I'd always had of a happy marriage and children of my own with the man I loved."

During a session with Hank, an idea came up for a symbolic "laying to rest" ceremony and to name my child, a customary right of all parents.

This idea didn't come from outside my mind but was entirely something that arose within me as a logical method for resolving some of my grief. It was an outgrowth of the realization that birth mothers traditionally submerge their grief in our society and that it is not recognized or appreciated for the most part, even by family and friends. So the seed for having a "Relinquishment Memorial" started here in my grief work with my therapist. My Catholic and psychiatric nurse background was part of its formation and subsequent planning.

Another assignment was to identify what was resolved adequately for me from the list.

*What's resolved enough:*

1. *Missed seeing her grow and change through the years and picking up Bock's family traits.*

2. *Missed seeing who she looks like — how she will carry my genes long after I'm gone.*

3. *I didn't get to know her, talk to her, or find out what she was — her personality, dreams, and talents.*

4. *I didn't get to play tennis with her, go shopping together, go garage sailing, or go out to lunch.*

12. *I missed seeing her dressed up for the prom.*

13. *I missed seeing her graduation.*

19. *I lost time and money when I took time off at the end of the pregnancy.*

*20. I lost nearness to my family when I left Kansas City to hide in Tulsa, and then from there followed the man I married there to Chicago.*

# The Decision to Go Ahead with Contact

Not having had a response to my ad for the registry in her hometown paper, I had no idea if Rose was interested in hearing from me. Of course, I had no luck with the Oklahoma state reunion registry because, in fact, and unknown to me at the time, the adoption took place in Kansas. Ironically had Rose wanted to find me, she could have requested her original, but an uncertified, birth certificate from the vital records office in Kansas upon turning 18. The original birth certificate had my name on it, a key clue for her search if only she had wanted to.

To my knowledge, at the time Rose turned 18, Kansas and Alaska were the only states allowing adult adoptees access to original birth certificates. Since then, more states have granted to adult adoptees, in varying degrees, more access to their original birth certificates and court adoption proceedings.

So, upon her turning 18 in April of 1987, I decided to contact her with the help of a pros and cons list.

*These are notes from my notebook:*

*When — near B.D. April 7*

*Pros: action is taken, and relief for me. Effect on Rose — unknown*

*Possible: interfere with final grades and tennis tournament*

*Con: effect on parents — negative likely, bad time due to normal break away occurring at 18 and mother's anxiety of losing a daughter*

*Possible pro*

*Rose and their parents welcome to contact, and Rose is able to assimilate knowledge of heritage into early adult personality*

*Con re: letter method*

*— allows recipient time to absorb content and react in private (this is not a con, but it is in my notes under con)*

*when — after BD, near graduation*

*Pro — same as for me and would avoid interference in Rose's grades*

It seems my pros and cons were related to when to contact rather than **if** to go ahead. By this time, I think I was chomping at the bit and ready to go forward now that she was 18.

Subsequently, I composed a letter and sent it by certified mail, the receipt of which I still have in my notebook. It was stamped Jun 1, 1987, and cost $2.92. On the receiving end, it required the addressee's signature (Rose). The receipt was returned to me and stamped Jun 4, 1987. With the returned receipt bearing Rose's signature, I knew that she had received it unless someone in her household signed her name in her place and never gave it to her. I rejected this as unlikely.

For the life of me, I cannot find a copy of the original letter I sent to her, which is surprising because I usually saved the most important documents related to Rose. I have searched my files, and everywhere it would logically be. Perhaps I sent my copy in the collected materials I sent to Rose a couple of years ago. I remember taking things out of my files, copying some of them and putting them in a notebook for her. In doing this, I may have forgotten, or even intentionally, given her a copy of the original letter I wrote, plus the response I received a year later from her mother on her behalf.

When I put together a large packet of materials for Rose, I recall thinking that I would finally stop asking her for a meeting. I believe I told her that with this accumulation of material and family history, including medical, I wouldn't be contacting her again. Of course, I didn't stick to this, but I remember at that time wanting resolution, an ending to my yearning, even if it meant no further contact from me. I was always whistling in the wind, hoping and praying for her to change her heart. I'd hoped that she would have some sympathy, some understanding of my situation, and want to help me, her birth mother.

But at that point, I had given up. I perhaps put the important letters in the files I sent her, thinking it was all over. My hope was dashed. I was surrendering in defeat. Whatever the reason for the first letter to her no longer being in my possession, I cannot say for sure.

I am sure that I told her in the letter that I thought she was the daughter I had placed for adoption on such and such date and time, the hospital where I gave birth, and a copy of the hospital record of her birth I had obtained during my search. I told her I was interested in meeting her and answering any questions she might have for me. I know I told her I was not trying to replace her adoptive parents, because I knew they were her "real" parents, the ones who raised and nurtured her.

# A Response from Rose, Actually From her Mother

I waited for months without a response of any kind. I recall sending another letter a year later asking for a response, but again, I can't find a copy of that one in my files.

But finally, I got a response. It was postmarked on August 23, 1988. I was married to my third husband by that time and had moved back to Missouri to be closer to family. My third husband, unlike my second, was supportive of my search. The return address said it was from Rose, but the majority of the letter inside was from her mother, not her, although she wrote a short note at the end saying she agreed with what her mother wrote.

It was written on lined, three-holed notebook paper. It was three and a half pages long.

*Here is the text:*

*Aug. 22, 1988*

*Judy Bock,*

*My name is Lucy .... and I am Rose's mother. I will respond to your letters and feel you will understand why as you read this letter.*

*First and foremost, Rose does not wish to communicate with you any further but wants you to know that she has never felt that your giving her up for adoption was a form of rejection or an unloving act, quite the contrary. From the time she was very small and through her growing years, it was explained to her, as she could understand in more detail, that the circumstances surrounding her birth did not turn out as you had hoped for, and in you caring for her best, you gave her up for adoption into a complete family.*

121

*We have Rose and an adopted son. They both have been taught that not being reared by their natural parents means, God has an extra special plan for their lives. (like Moses) That God chose the right parents and environment for the goals He wants them to achieve. They both have reassurance of God's loving — leading in their lives by bringing them into this family. They know they are special.*

*During the last month of school preceding Rose's graduation, as she received any honors and awards and as I observed how she is admired by young and old alike, for her many outstanding qualities ... I often thought of you and wanted you to know what a fine young lady she is and is still becoming ...*

*Rose is strong in character, secure, contented, and has a healthy self-image and a grateful heart. She is loyal, truthful (very open), obedient (never was she rebellious), sincere, diligent, responsible, intelligent, wise for her age, self-disciplined, resourceful, determined, decisive and full of initiative, and has a bubbly, witty, charming personality. She is also beautiful in physical appearance, and as I and many others feel, this is one thing that makes her so exceptional ... That combination of outward and inward beauty (kindness, humility, unpretentiousness, self-acceptance etc ...)*

*She has a mother and father that believe "family is first." She has a special relationship with her father — they are so much alike in every way. She and her brother have always been close. We come from a very large and close family.*

*Rose's Grandparents, Aunts, Uncles, Cousins, etc., all love her and hold her in close esteem.*

*To others, Rose speaks freely and with pride concerning her adoption. She was told at approximately 13 if she wanted to know more about her natural parents or wanted to find them for any reason, we would help make that available for her. She expressed then, as she does now, "I do not wish or need to do that."*

*As you can conclude, the reason I wrote the letter is #1 to tell you of Rose's wishes: She does not need or desire to know you or communicate with you concerning the circumstances surrounding her adoption. #2 to tell you what a unique and special person she is and that she has a great environment to grow up and live in.*

*In closing, I wish to say Rose and I want and pray you will be unburdened and at peace about your decision of 19 years ago. Your decision from Rose's side has been a very blessed one.*

*Sincerely, Lucy ……*

The following is an addendum from Rose.

*Judy Bock* (notably, I am not "dear")

*I have read this letter and share the same feelings as my mother. I do not hold any grudges toward you, and I think your decision to give me up for adoption was best. I do not wish to continue any further communication with you because I feel it would be damaging to my family and me.*

*Sincerely,*

*Rose*

My response to this rejection letter to meet me was one of profound disappointment; however, I don't recall being devastated or slumping into a depressed state. Perhaps I was in denial that this could possibly be the true desire of my daughter. I thought she might not want to upset her parents by starting a relationship with me.

Friends and close relations told me that she was probably heavily influenced by her mother, who, although expressing willingness to abide by whatever Rose wanted, truly didn't wish to share her daughter with me. To Rose and her family, this would likely be the end of it, and they wouldn't hear from me again.

That wasn't the case. I continued in my persistent quest with periodic contact through the years.

# I Pressed On

I have a framed work of calligraphy that now hangs above my computer desk and has been an inspiration to me through my search for Rose, my pursuit of a journalism degree and other goals that have been challenging to achieve. The inspirational piece is one by former U.S. President Calvin Coolidge, and I considered it worthy of framing and displaying in a place I would often see.

In addition to the above pep talk that I frequently looked at, I was bolstered in my thinking after reading numerous articles, books, and personal testimonies at conferences and during triad support group meetings that there is seemingly a universal desire by adoptees to know about their biological background and, in addition, a yearning to meet their birth parents, in particular their birth mothers.

Therefore, in a true sense, I was still hopeful that there would be an eventual change in Rose's desire to meet me or at least maintain some form of communication in lieu of an actual meeting.

I found it interesting that Rose's parents offered to make more information available to her when she was 13, about the time I'd asked the obstetrician's office to send a letter to them from me.

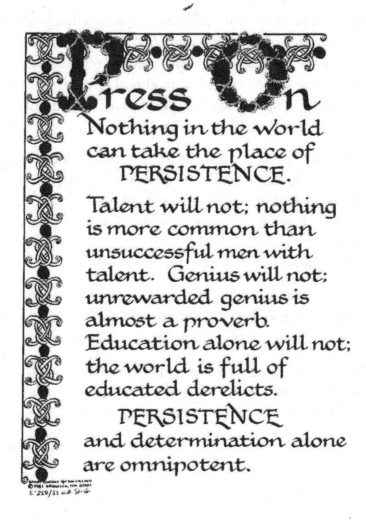

Press On

Nothing in the world
can take the place of
PERSISTENCE.

Talent will not; nothing
is more common than
unsuccessful men with
talent. Genius will not;
unrewarded genius is
almost a proverb.
Education alone will not;
the world is full of
educated derelicts.

PERSISTENCE
and determination alone
are omnipotent.

*A quote by former President Calvin Coolidge hangs above my office desk.*

# The Relinquishment Memorial

Today I truly don't think I am fooling myself that I have, for the most part, arrived at a feeling of resolution and acceptance regarding my loss of Rose Diane. But over 10 years after contacting her and receiving the letter of refusal to meet from Rose and her mother, I must have still been working on accepting my loss. So I planned and held what I called a Relinquishment Memorial.

As previously noted, I arrived at the idea during counseling with Hank. I got the message that I needed to figure out how to heal myself meaningfully.

Having been raised Roman Catholic, the concept of a ceremonial ritual to mark an important life event was familiar. Baptism, confirmation, marriage, and other sacraments and rituals of the church marked spiritual growth and acknowledgment of something important in the lives of the faithful.

When someone in the Catholic faith dies, a special Mass is often followed by a burial at a cemetery where the priest has set prayers and actions that have been passed down in the church's traditions through the centuries.

I felt that some sort of ceremony of sorts might be a way to acknowledge my loss and my family's loss of this child. I think some people considered it pretty weird, but it was a good thing.

I had forgotten until looking at the date on the invitation again that I had scheduled it on my birthday, which was preceded the day before by Rose Diane's. The weather was likely to be mild and spring-like, and it turned out that way.

You are cordially invited to a

Relinquishment Memorial to acknowledge

the loss to adoption in 1969

of the infant daughter of Judith Bock

2:00 p.m. April 8, 2001

Our Lady of Peace Monastery

Columbia, Missouri

Lunch and reception to follow

RSVP to Judith at 573-449-0924

*Above is a copy of my relinquishment memorial invitation.*

My sister Barbara was a member of the Benedictine community of sisters that lived at a small monastery of Benedictine nuns in Columbia, Missouri. She was both my sister and a close friend. We had fun together, including traveling cross country, biking on numerous trails, organizing and joining family canoe trips and playing highly competitive Scrabble. The other nuns were willing to share their monastery, a place big enough for around 30-40 people in their meeting room.

The memorial started with my testimony about my history as a birth parent and continued with a description of my search and why I decided to have a relinquishment memorial. I spoke at a podium while those who attended sat in chairs.

### My Memorial Testimony

*I want to thank you all for coming and sharing this time with me. It means a lot. As some of you know, this relinquishment memorial is a result of some counseling I received over a period of several months last year.*

*Hank, my counselor, encouraged me to work on my unresolved grief over the loss of the child I had in 1969 and soon after relinquished for adoption. I knew this was a core issue in my life, the most devastating event that had occurred in my 53 years. Subsequent infertility after the relinquishment was a major strain on two of my previous marriages that ended in divorce.*

*The idea of having others share my loss with me in a public way appealed to me. Because of the shame and embarrassment of getting pregnant and not being married, even in the liberal 60s, I hid away and had my baby out of state, in Oklahoma, and didn't tell most of my family until years later. My psychiatric nursing experience taught me that sharing grief with others can be healing. I announced to Hank that I wished to have a relinquishment memorial for the infant I lost and that I was going to think of a name to give her as an infant. Hank thought it a good idea.*

*I spent several days, maybe a week, coming up with a name. Finally, I chose Rose Diane. I chose Rose as a first name because many beloved people in my life have Rose as a first or second name and for the name of a most beautiful flower. The second name, Diane, is to honor my friend from nursing school, who was my roommate and my main support person during my pregnancy and when I gave birth. She was in the delivery room in Tulsa and is the only person I now know who saw baby Rose. I was given medications that blocked my memory of the delivery.*

*Having named my baby has been a comfort to me. I can now more easily separate the infant, Rose, that was mine, from the person of xxxxx, who is someone else's child. To have this separation is important because it helps me accept what is not mine, but to acknowledge that she **actually was** my baby daughter. When I see a rose in a design, in pictures, or in a garden, I am touched with a warm feeling as I think of Rose Diane.*

*I am blessed with support from everyone who matters to me, including my dear husband, Glenn, and all of you who are here today. It feels liberating to finally have everyone in my family in on this part of my life. I also recognize that Rose was not only my loss but also a loss to the Bock family as a whole. Because she was an Oklahoma State tennis finalist in high school, she possibly could have beaten her cousin Danny Bock, who always gave me a hard time for losing against him. I thank the sisters of Our Lady of Peace Monastery for letting me have this the ceremony here today, and especially my sister Barbara who helped with all aspects of it.*

*I've prepared a document with Rose's name and birth statistics that we will bury today, along with some rose petals from Dad's funeral bouquet. He had wanted to meet her someday, but it wasn't to be in this life. Perhaps we can all meet her at a Bock reunion in heaven someday.*

*We will plant a rose bush in the same place as the document. To me, this will symbolize a new life beginning after her separation from me. After the burial, we will go in and have lunch, and I will share my library of documents, letters and pictures that I've accumulated during my search and attempted reunion with Rose.*

*But first, we will have a prayer, and then all join in on a song.*

*Thank you.*

As I read the prepared testimony at the memorial to my family and friends gathered there, I was struck by how some were crying, including my niece, Paula, who had come to the memorial despite a terrible cold. Although I could read the testimony without getting emotional, I felt lifted up and understood by the group gathered there.

Most profound of all was a simple comment my normally reserved mother said to me. It was sometime after I read my testimony, and I was passing near where she sat. Our eyes met, and she said very simply, "Judy, I'm very proud of you." She had never spoken those words to me before, all during my school years, even at graduations or other milestones of accomplishment. But to hear it now … well, it was what I needed. Thanks, Mom. Perhaps I had not heard it before because she and Dad had the German characteristic of parenting with firm discipline and not wanting to "give us big heads."

## Memorial Prayer

*Oh, heavenly Father, we come to you in prayer.*

*We ask for your healing of the wounds of separation.*

*Give us peace as we travel the paths we are now on.*

*We know you are with us.*

*Help us to remember we are not alone in our sorrow.*

*Guide us as we strive for our new beginnings.*

*Lord, be with all unmarried pregnant women and girls who must decide the fate of their unborn.*

*Bless them with courage to do your will.*

*Help them to reach out to those you have placed here who can help them the most.*

*Bless the fathers of these unborn, that they too may do your will. Forgive those who do not, and help us to forgive them as well.*

*Lord, bless the adopted, that they may know the love and bonding of good family life.*

*Let them be open to knowing their families of origin.*

*Bless their parents with an understanding*

*of their need to know their roots.*

*We thank you for the many blessings of love in our families and in the Friendships that we have in our lives today.*

*Amen*

Soon after my testimony and prayer, I invited everyone to come out to the garden area of the monastery to plant the rose bush and birth document I'd prepared. The document was a simple statement of Rose's name, date of birth, parents' names, and the hospital and city of her birth.

Although I believe this event was important and effective in helping me resolve some of the grief of losing my baby, not everyone thought it was such a good idea. I got comments from one friend who obviously thought it was over the top and not something I'd ever want to tell Rose about. He characterized it as a burial, something associated with death.

I buried that document and planted the rose bush and rose petals from dad's funeral bouquet as a symbolic gesture of putting the loss behind me and giving respect to my dad. But it was also a recognition of Rose's adoption. As stated in my testimony that I read, planting the rose bush was symbolic of her continued life away from me. Not living at the monastery, I could not control the life of that rose bush, nor nourish and care for it as that was under the duties of one of the nuns, just as Rose was being cared for by her adoptive family and not within my control or authority in any way.

I remember my husband Glenn and stepdaughter Melissa assisting in planting the rose bush. Glenn's reassuring presence and active participation were strong supports that were really helpful, as they are to this day. He had never wavered from his understanding of my need to grieve this loss, having himself suffered the tragic loss of his first wife in a car accident when his children were still young.

After we planted the rose bush, I invited anyone who wished to pour some water on it from a watering can. Like sacramental baptism in the Christian tradition, blessing with water is a sacred and symbolic ritual testifying to new life. Several stepped up and said a few words as they poured a bit of water on the plant.

I fondly recall my niece Kathy, herself an adoptive mother, saying heartfelt and meaningful words as she poured water on the new rose bush and buried documents.

We then went back into the monastery, where we shared lunch.

I felt I had given some closure and dignity to my loss of my infant daughter. Today, the rose bush burial place is part of an apartment complex built after the nuns sold the monastery and grounds and dispersed to other communities within the Benedictine order of nuns.

Much like the rose bush, I truly had no control over the course of Rose's life after her adoption.

# Recorded Phone Calls and a Letter After Finding Rose

The idea of recording these calls probably occurred because I had been used to doing this during interviews in journalism school and afterward in my free-lance writing interviews. I had some old cassette tapes labeled as phone calls to Rose but only spoke with her husband Richard in March of 2003 and a few weeks later, on March 18 of 2003 with Rose.

### Transcription of the first call with Richard:

*The phone rings once: Man's voice says, "Hello." Judy: Hello, is this Richard?*

*Richard: Yes*

*Judy: This is Judy Bock. I don't know if you're familiar with that name.*

*Richard: Yeah? Go ahead.*

*Judy: I sincerely apologize if this is an intrusion or a bad time to talk…(pause)*

*Richard: I'm not sure who you are.*

*Judy: I'm Rose's birth mother.*

*Richard: Okay*

*Judy: I'm actually calling to speak with Rose, but perhaps I could talk to you a little bit.*

*Richard: She's not here. I don't feel comfortable talking to you until I talk to her about it.*

*Judy: Sure, I understand. Is there a time I could call back?*

*Richard: She's actually out of town for a week.*

*Judy: I see. Maybe I could give you an idea of why I'm calling, and you could talk to her about it. Ummm…*(probably trying to figure out what to say next) *I'm going to be making a trip down to that part of northwest Arkansas towards the end of the month, and I'm going to be around Eureka Springs and Fort Smith. I used to go to school at St. Scholastica's in Fort Smith. (cleared throat) And I just thought… umm … I mean, I'm quite aware she doesn't want a relationship or anything, but I just thought I would just check…sometimes people change their minds about contact and things. I just thought I'd ask if she'd be interested in meeting me at least one time in my life.*

*Richard: OK. Why don't you give me your number, and I will leave her a note because I'll be out of town when she gets back.*

*Judy: I see.*

*Richard: Where can she reach you?*

*Judy:* (I gave my phone number, and he repeated it.) *I'm usually here in the evenings or on Tuesdays, usually during the day.*

*Richard: OK*

*Judy: Well, I appreciate you talking to me.*

*Richard: I will leave her this note, and she can decide what she wants to do.*

*Judy: OK, thanks*

*Richard: OK (Call ended)*

**Follow-up call with Rose on 3-18-2003**

The recording began sometime after the conversation started:

*Rose: ...but someday I probably would like to.* (This apparently is her response to my request for meeting face to face.)

*Judy: Okay, well, whenever it seems like the right time. That would be great. I don't want to push you.*

*Rose: I have a...mostly just ... because I feel it would be hard on my parents that raised me. So...*

*Judy: Yeah. Well, I know that's something that adopted persons are concerned about. And they're your real parents, the people that raised you. So... but a... you are the only child I ever had ... I know I am not ... can never be your parent; they're your parents. But someday, I would like to meet you face to face, at least once.*

*Rose: Oh ... Yeah ... I uh ... like I said, I could do it; the timing right now is just not ... not good for me.*

*Judy: Okay.*

*Rose: Richard said you would be in town at the end of the month, maybe ...*

*Judy: Well, I'm going to visit ... well, I'm not sure if I will be able to make the trip with my mother being so sick. I expected to visit a longtime friend who lives in Tulsa ... in fact, she was a person who was at your birth...Diane. I lived with her when I was pregnant with you. And we were going to go to Eureka Springs and then maybe down to Fort Smith. I went to school at a boarding school at St. Scholastica's. I don't know if you've ever heard of it.*

*Rose: No, I haven't.*

*Judy: In Fort Smith. It's a Catholic boarding school. And a ... so ... I hadn't been down there in a while and thought I'd be so close ... I thought I'd give you a chance ... just in case you'd changed your mind.*

*Rose: So, is your religious background Catholic?*

*Judy: Yes, I was raised Catholic. I'm still practicing, but I'm certainly open to other religions... I wasn't a practicing Catholic when I placed you for adoption, so I didn't specify, you know, anything about what the adoptive parents should be.*

*Rose: Right ... Richard's sister and her family are Catholic. But we go to a Southern Baptist Church.*

*Judy: Baptist? Uh-huh, yeah ...*

*Rose: I've been in several different denominations or non-denominations growing up.*

*Judy: Uh-huh, yeah, I've done a little bit of religious exploration, I guess you'd say and always am. The Catholic Church is pretty, you know, dogmatic at times ... and paternalistic... but it's my family's religion, so ... and my husband became a Catholic not too long ago. It's kind of a unifying thing, I guess.*

*Rose: I don't know too much about it.*

*Judy: Anyway ... do you have children?*

*Rose: Uh-huh, we have four.*

*Judy: Oh my gosh, you've been busy since I talked with you last* (playful tone and chuckle).

*Rose: Yeah, we have four, and that was the other aspect of it. I'm not real comfortable with that. They don't know. I mean, they know I'm adopted, but they don't know... I think that would be confusing for them right now.*

*Judy: Uh-huh.*

*Rose: I don't know... I just haven't thought of all the ... oh, what's the word I'm looking for ... how it would affect them, I guess.*

*Judy: Ramifications maybe ... well, umm*

*Rose: On the top of my head ... I had a list of questions once Richard told me, but I can't think of any of them right now.*

*Judy: Okay... well umm ... if you'd like to call sometime ... or write ... I have an email.*

*Rose: I was going to ask you if you have an email account. Mine is ...@juneau.com.*

*Judy: Okay...* (repeated Rose's email) *... all lowercase? I'm* jbock@xxxx.org.

*Rose: jbock? I didn't hear you*

*Judy:* jbock@xxxx.org

*Rose: Okay.*

*Judy:* (cleared throat) *... So you can email me your questions ... I just don't want to pressure you, but I'm open to whatever you feel comfortable with regarding contact.*

*Rose: All I can do is put myself in your shoes, in the position you were in, and I'd probably be doing the same thing, but ...*

*Judy: Well, I appreciate you saying that. But of course, I've had regrets, as I think my letter probably indicated, and sometimes I wished I'd contacted your parents first, so they could have gotten an idea of what kind of person I am. And, of course, if things were the way they are now with birth parents, I would have wanted to meet them before I placed you for adoption. There are many things I would have changed. I would have wanted to have seen you. I never got to see you* (voice breaks a little and with a sad tone.)

*Rose: That's one reason I would have liked for you to have seen ... maybe the kids ... it could have given you an indication of what I would have looked like. (laughs a little.)*

*Judy: Well, I'm glad you had kids. That's neat ... so ... anyway, but I'm married. I have a stepdaughter now. I married a younger man, so ... I've got a teenager, which is a little much for me right now, but she's not bad as teenagers go.*

*Rose:* (slight laugh) *I haven't gotten to that phase yet. Not too much longer ... (cleared her throat) ... anyway, we just walked in the door from Sam's, and I've got some frozen things.*

*Judy: Oh dear, you better get ... I'll let you go.*

*Rose: So I better get in there. But I'm glad you called.*

*Judy: It was great talking to you. I'm encouraged that you might someday feel comfortable, and maybe we can email for a while and see how things go ... or whatever.*

*Rose: Okay.*

*Judy: All right, Rose, I'll let you go. Get that stuff in the refrigerator* ... (laughs)

*Rose: Okay, thanks.*

*Judy: Okay, bye.*

*Rose: Bye.* (end of the call)

I'm not sure why I delayed starting the taping after the call started, as I am the one who initiated the call. Her comment confirms this about needing to get frozen stuff put away and "I'm glad you called." With the date of 3-18 on the tape, I think I must have felt some urgency to know her decision so that I could make trip plans. Plus, it had been 15 days since the call with Richard, with no response from her.

This was our second phone conversation, the first being during her senior year at Baylor, which I documented elsewhere. I can't say that I was keeping up with her life, as I didn't know she had four children. Many years later, when Facebook became available, I got a better look at some of the important events of her life.

Rose was open and forthcoming with her address and other information on both calls. In my search efforts, however, I was able to find out a lot without her telling me. It wasn't until I met her in person that I learned she felt alone in her decision to meet me or give me information finally. She told me that Richard was very private and didn't want people, probably especially me, to know much about their personal lives. So she was brave and assertive in following her own desires. I admire this in her.

### Letter from Rose 12-10-03

This letter, which I received about nine months after our most recent phone conversation, gives a good picture of why Rose didn't feel ready to meet me or get into a relationship that would add even more stress to her life.

*Dear Judy,*

*I'm still not at ease with starting a face-to-face relationship, but I wanted you to have a Christmas card from me anyway. I had good intentions to write or e-mail you earlier, but we have had one setback after another. Since our last conversation, our house has flooded due to a pipe bursting. We were out of our home for weeks and not back to normal for months while they repaired sheetrock, painted, and replaced carpet and tile throughout the house.*

*Next, we found out Richard's dad had acute leukemia and is still fighting in his 3$^{rd}$ round going into 4$^{th}$ round of treatment. We have traveled to see him quite a bit, as well as a trip to Florida and Colorado for family and vacation visits. Finally, I just had surgery for hernias and other complications and have had a slow recovery back to health.*

*So, as you now know, things have been a little hectic — not to mention homeschooling the children and teaching my son's 4$^{th}$ grade Sunday school class at church. Hopefully, after the holidays, life will slow down enough for me to relax a bit and focus on other areas of my life. I hope you are well and haven't had this flu going around. It's epidemic here. So far, only Richard has had it. Have a merry Christmas, and I'll write again.*

*Sincerely, Rose*

The Christmas card was one of those picture postcards that people often send around the holidays. It was of her four young children running happily on a beach, no doubt in Florida, during the family vacation that year. I remember being thrilled to get the card. I scrutinized the images of the children to see if I saw any family resemblance. I did not. The image was not the clearest, but I suspect the kids, except the oldest, mostly got their looks from their father's side.

Sending this card was a kind and generous thing for Rose to do, and I am grateful for this gesture. I have the photograph framed and on the wall in my office, among other photos of my family.

Upon looking at their images on the card, I did not feel instant love for these children, my biological grandchildren. I felt, and continue to feel, a high degree of detachment. This disappoints me in a way, but it's the truth. Perhaps it's the same emotional detachment or hardening I had learned early in my life to protect me from psychological trauma. But then, maybe I am over-analyzing. I had tried to make this detachment work for me at the time I placed Rose for adoption, a detachment that shattered when I awoke to the enormity of my loss years later.

# Open Adoption: my Niece's Real-Life Experience

Contrasted with my own experience with a closed adoption, one in which the identities of the adoption triad are kept secret, was my niece Kathy's and her husband Rick's open adoption of their two daughters. I will focus on that of their younger daughter, Gina.

Kathy and Rick had adopted their first child, Melia, a few years earlier and wanted to try to adopt another child, having considered it such a wonderful experience. However, they had just about decided to call off their quest to adopt again after a roller coaster of emotional ups and downs with six prospective adoptions that failed to reach completion.

They were on lots of adoption registries but were about to call it quits when a social worker called them one mid-August day. She asked if she could give their file to a young woman who wanted to place her newborn in an adoptive home. Soon after agreeing, they went to the hospital for an in-person interview with the newborn's mother, Sara. She had already interviewed two other couples.

Sara wanted her daughter to have an older sibling and a household with a dog and plans to provide private schooling. Kathy and Rick could only promise the first of these criteria, but they got chosen anyway. Sara told them later that it was because of the impression she got as soon as they walked in the door.

Kathy elaborates on what Sara told her about that first encounter: "She told us that she liked how we walked in together, held hands, sat close to each other and seemed in sync with each other." She went on to tell Kathy, "You gave me a big hug before leaving and told me that 'Whatever you choose will be just fine." Kathy had no recollection of the hug and the "Whatever you choose" statement, but knowing her as I do as her "sister-aunt," this would have been typical of her kindness. They got a call the next day that they were the chosen parents.

"Sara told us that she thought we would be able to tell our daughter how much her birth mother had loved her," Kathy added. This was emphatically evident when, seven days after her birth, Kathy and Rick came to pick up Gina from the hospital. Although Sara had been discharged on day two post-delivery, she had arrived at the nursery and been with Gina from morning until visiting hours ended each day.

Kathy described picking up Gina as a time of peak elation for her and Rick; however, it was the extreme opposite for Sara. "Gina was in a bassinet in a room at the hospital. As we rolled her down the hall, we could hear Sara in the room behind us wailing pitifully and loudly as we took Gina away. I felt her broken heart; at the same time, mine was filled with joy. So yes, I had a good idea of the depth of her love for our Gina."

Knowing how much Sara truly wanted her baby and loved her, Kathy and Rick were extremely fearful when they learned she would be attending the court hearing for the final adoption proceedings. "There was some talk that the birth father might be coming as well," Kathy said. "We had fallen in love with this baby after bonding with her for one and a half months. We were seriously ready to hop in the car and drive into Canada to keep her in the event Sara had changed her mind and wanted her back."

"We imagined her having gotten back with the birth father with plans to marry him and wanting to claim their baby." But it turned out that she had come to make a statement in support of Kathy and Rick as Gina's new parents. "She was dressed in a suit and looked beautiful," Kathy remembered.

As promised, they sent Sara photos and updates of Gina's progress every six months for about three years until the letters with enclosed photos started coming back as undeliverable.

During Gina's growing up years, she knew she was adopted and that her birth mother had loved her. "She didn't ask us many questions about her first mother until she was around 15 years old," Kathy said.

At the time of her adoption, Sara had given us a letter, pictures of her family and a music box to be shared with Gina when she was ready for them. So, when Gina started asking questions, Kathy said to her, "Remember, you have pictures, a letter and a music box stored in your bedroom closet from your birth mother."

Because updated letters and photos had been returned due to the address being invalid since Gina was three years old, her parents had no current information to share with their inquiring teen. Here is where Gina took things into her own hands.

Gina went to her closet and found the music box, letter and photos. As she examined the music box, a piece of paper revealed a receipt with Sara's name and address at the time of purchase.

Five months later, Gina took a big step at a slumber party in her quest to find her birth mother. With a search on Facebook, she could locate a woman by the right name who had been living in the Kansas City area at the time of Gina's birth.

Kathy recalls that soon after the slumber party Gina came to them and said she had something important to tell them. She was in tears, Kathy recalled, but valiantly went forward. "I have something to tell you, and you might not like it," Gina said. Kathy and Rick started to cry with her, and Kathy related that it was "a momentous-spine-tingling moment," as Gina told them of her search and finding Sara on Facebook. "At that time and throughout Gina's life, we were very aware how much Sara loved her and how much it took to give her up," Kathy said they assured Gina.

Rick had some concerns that many adoptive parents voiced who have protective responses to the involvement of the birth family in their children's lives. These were about potential interference in the lives of the adoptive family.

As it turned out, these fears were greatly reduced after Gina and her parents met with Sara and later her husband and three children. Gina and Sara, along with her children and husband, bonded quickly. The bonding that developed was evident when Gina included Sara and her family in her wedding party years later. Her half-sister was even a bridesmaid.

Sara gave a touching toast at the wedding reception and told the other guests about her gratitude for Gina being adopted by such wonderful parents. A few years later, Gina also met her birth father and his wife and began another extended family relationship. The latter, however, caused major friction between Gina and Sara and is yet to be resolved at this writing. As I learned through my research into triad reunions and my own experience, many post-reunions have their ups and downs.

In my viewpoint, Gina's adoption is the ideal of the open adoption concept. There are many adoptions with varying degrees of openness with differing responses to reunions and continued connections. In most published stories of reunions among triad members from closed and open adoptions, the responses are overwhelmingly positive in favor of openness. Of course, I focused on these as they confirmed what I hoped for myself. I did hear less favorable reports from time to time at adoption conferences about adoptees and birth parents who refused or initially resisted contact or forming relationships. No doubt these unhappy stories don't make it to publishing outlets as often as the feel-good ones with happy endings.

Without a doubt, I was hoping to capture some of the success I observed Gina and her birth family achieve in my quest to reunite with Rose.

# An Adoptee's Viewpoint of Reuniting with Birth Family

After talking to her mother, I talked to my niece Gina about her experience of reuniting with her birth family. She echoed much of what her mother reported.

I asked Gina why she wanted to find and meet her birth family.

"I'd been thinking about it for a long time before I acted on it. I was 15 at the time," Gina, who was in her late 20's at the time of her interview with me, said. "Finding my birth family was something I really wanted to do. So I eventually asked my mom what she knew about my birth mom one day. In addition to other information, she reminded me of the jewelry box from Sara that was stored in my closet." Kathy had described it as a music box with a little ballerina figurine that would pirouette when opened. It was big enough to hold some jewelry.

"So I went to the shelf in my closet and got the box down, and on the underside was a receipt for it with Sara's full name at the time she bought it along with her email and phone number."

Kathy had told me that Gina had apparently played with it a lot through the years, as it showed some wear. Apparently, Gina had not earlier discovered or realized the significance of the receipt and its connection to her birth mother.

She told me that Gina's detective work started in earnest and moved quickly. Although Sara's contact information on the receipt had changed since the jewelry box was purchased, Gina was able to piece together information from the receipt and connect the right person with the timeline on Facebook with a good amount of certainty.

"One day, I got on Facebook and messaged the person I thought was her. I was so excited and nervous when I got a response that very night. I was at a friend's house at a slumber party when I got it." Sara responded by returning a Facebook message that Gina was a good detective and that, yes, she was her birth mother. I can only imagine the excitement at that slumber party.

Gina didn't tell her parents right away that night, but the next day she asked them to come and sit down with her, that she had something to tell them. "I was a bit worried that mom would be upset about it, but she wasn't. Dad was concerned from a protective standpoint, not wanting me to get hurt."

Gina told me about the face-to-face reunion that occurred two months later at Gina's home. Sara, who lives in the southwest United States, came to Gina's home with her sister Amy who lives in the Kansas City area. Amy had emotionally supported her through her pregnancy and adoption, which is why Gina's birth was in a Kansas City hospital.

"We were all pretty nervous waiting for them to come into the house," Gina said. She speculated that Sara and her sister were nervous as well. The nervous people waiting inside the home, namely Kathy, Rick and Gina, were scared Sara and Amy would decide to leave because they sat in Amy's car in the driveway for what seemed an eternity.

Finally, they got out of the car and came to the front door where Gina, in tears by this time, was waiting with her parents standing close by. Kathy and Rick stood back while Gina and Sara hugged for a very long time, both crying.

Eventually, the rest of the family were introduced to each other, and the visit continued with Gina, Sara and Amy sitting in a front room while Kathy and Rick busied themselves in the kitchen preparing a meal. Kathy remembered hearing laughter from them and knew the reunion was off to a good start. The visit continued through and after dinner for quite a while. It concluded with an invitation to return, more hugs and promises to keep in touch.

I was eventually fortunate to meet Sara when she and Amy came to Gina's high school graduation party in Kathy and Rick's home. I spoke to Sara about her feelings about meeting Gina and learning about her life in her adoptive family. "Although I am happy to be a part of Gina's life now," she said somberly, "I am sad about missing so much of her growing-up years."

Sara had brought a large photo album to the graduation party containing photos of that first week of Gina's life while still in the hospital and waiting for her placement with an adoptive family. Although Sara had been discharged two days after Gina's birth, she returned every morning to be with her as soon as visitors were allowed. She held and fed her and stayed until the visitors' hours ended at night. The album's photos from this time were on display for anyone to look at while they attended the party. I paged through it and marveled at seeing a smiling, healthy baby who Sara had the privilege to hold, love and nurture for the first week of life.

I remember thinking how fortunate Sara was to have been able to hold her baby and to further the bond that had formed before birth. It deserves repeating that it would have been more difficult for me emotionally to have relinquished Rose to her adoptive parents had I bonded with my baby as Sara had, but I think it would have been worth it to have had this irretrievable time with Rose.

# I Wish You Would!

One day, I said to my longtime trusted friend Cindy, "I think I'll give Rose a call and tell her I'm going to be driving by her house on my way to my sister's in Fort Smith and was just wondering if I could stop in or maybe meet her somewhere as I drive nearby." I said this tongue in cheek, as it was a preposterous proposition to be sure.

Cindy paused a while, looked directly into my eyes and without blinking said in a very emphatic serious way, "I wish you would!" and then she repeated, "I sure wish you would!"

Her summons for action reverberated in my brain for most of the rest of that day. It was still playing over and over in my head until I began to think that I would go ahead and call her.

I said a prayer, picked up my phone and dialed Rose's number.

It felt rather surreal. Was I really doing this? I had jumped off the bridge, maybe with a bungee cord, to be able to hang up. But she answered after only a few rings.

"Hello, Rose, this is Judy Bock, and I know I've asked you numerous times, but I'm heading your way in the next few days, and I just thought I'd ask one more time if you want to meet," I blurted out in one breath.

A slight pause, then "Can you hold on a minute?" During that minute, I imagined her going to a different location in her home for more privacy.

Then I heard a live phone click on. "When are you coming?" she said. At this, my heart did somersaults in hopefulness. She hadn't immediately rejected the notion, I realized. In fact, she asked a question as if to see if she could possibly fit it into her calendar.

This is insane, I thought to myself. Maybe I'm dreaming. "I'm driving to Fort Smith this Friday for my eighth-grade teacher's wake and funeral. I'm probably coming home on Sunday," I told her.

"I might be able to meet you Sunday," she said, and my heart did a cartwheel.

"I was just at a program at my church the other night about abortion," she began. "It made me think of you and how maybe the woman who goes through with the pregnancy deserves to meet her child."

"But I'll have to think about it some more," she said.

"Yes, by all means, think about it, pray about it, talk to people you trust, and get back to me," I responded. This was Tuesday, so there really wasn't a lot of time.

"I'll get back to you in the next couple of days with an answer," Rose said. "Okay, great. I sure hope your answer will be yes," I said.

When I hung up, to say I was exhilarated was a gross understatement. I was rocketed to the moon, and she hadn't even said yes.

I don't know who I told first, but it was probably Cindy, as Glenn was at work. I either texted, emailed or called others of my friends and family to tell them to put this on their prayer lists for Rose to say yes.

I was taking my time packing Thursday when the phone rang, and the caller ID said it was from Rose. Were my prayers and all those of friends and relatives really being answered in the way we requested?

"No one but me thinks it's a good idea, but I can meet you this Friday at a fast-food place near my home at about 11:30. I have a

153

sports event my youngest is in, and I promised myself I would try to go to as many of her events as I can. So I only have about an hour before I'll have to leave and get to her game. Would you be able to meet me then?"

My mind was racing. A quick calculation told me I'd need to leave much earlier Friday morning than I'd originally planned in order to meet her that early. "Yes, of course, I'll get there," I said without thinking further. I don't remember what else we might have said, something about how the particular fast food franchise didn't have much to eat that's healthy, but maybe a salad or two.

When I got off the phone, I must have made a few phone calls or texts to announce the good news, but I am sure my mind was in overdrive. I'd need to pack and be ready to leave by 5 a.m., meaning I'd need to get to bed early and try to sleep if possible.

# The Meeting

I don't think I slept too soundly that night, but I was on the road by 5 a.m. Weather predictions called for rain and thunderstorms throughout much of my driving itinerary.

I had eaten a quick breakfast but didn't plan to stop much along the way except as needed for gas or restroom facilities.

The thunderstorm became intense as I approached the usually very busy highway that intersected that part of the state where Rose lived. Because it went through the fringes of several cities, including the one Rose lived in, it was about five lanes going one direction and five lanes going the other. I had never driven through that part of the state when this highway was not under construction somewhere. That day it was narrowed to three lanes or so, and the traffic was heavy as the noon hour was picking up.

I was feeling nervous about getting there on time. Just the immensity of meeting her would have been enough to occupy my mind, but I was focused on the immediate need to stay razor-sharp behind the wheel through torrents of heavy rain, almost obscuring my vision of the road and traffic ahead. Added to the mix, there was thunder and lightning. If I had believed that God was directly intervening in my plans and trying to make things difficult, I would have been just a bit upset with him/her.

But somehow, I made it to a gas station a few miles from the designated meeting spot, was able to use the restroom and caught my breath. The skies started clearing, and I was feeling confident I'd make it on time. I texted her from the gas station and told her I'd be there shortly. She texted me that she was already there and was accompanied by a dear friend of hers.

I wish I had known she was bringing a friend, and I could have had a support person with me as well. My nieces Paula and Kathy had expressed a desire to be with me. Kathy would have been an appropriate addition as an adoptive mom herself, whose daughters had both had varying degrees of contact with their birth mothers. Paula would have added vitality and humor to the situation, as was her special talent. My long-time friend Diane, who had been in the delivery room during Rose's birth, could have been there as she lived about a two-and-a-half-hour drive away and had also wanted to come.

So I was a bit blindsided by her friend's presence. I understand it from Rose's side, in that she needed a support person there whom she could trust to understand her emotions. I had the same needs and another set of ears to listen and help remember the conversation.

Having refreshed myself with a few minutes of rest at the gas station and realizing I wasn't late, I proceeded to the designated meeting place with an unusually controlled feeling of confidence and expectation.

Pulling into a parking spot, I noted the rain was letting up, and I was grateful for that. I felt amazingly calm. It seemed I should be more excited about finally meeting my long-lost daughter. I'd hoped and yearned for this, gone to numerous conferences to learn about it, devoured dozens of books and probably hundreds of articles, had many discussions with friends, relatives, strangers, and reporters, and I was ... calm. I felt enveloped by something outside myself, or maybe it was from something coming from within and a determination to complete something.

I gathered the sack of gifts and photographs I had gathered to give or show Rose and walked to the door of the building. Through the large windows, I could see a young woman wearing a purple plaid shirt Rose told me she'd be wearing. The woman was about my height with long, curly brown hair.

I entered the restaurant and focused on the young woman approaching me. Her arms were open, and I believe she was smiling, although this moment is already fading from memory. When I returned her welcoming embrace, I registered that this was the first time I had ever held my child and said as much, "This is the first time I have ever held you."

She introduced me to her friend Janice and explained that she had known her for many years and that she had been a mentor to her from her early days of teaching at their church school. They attended the same church and were in the same Bible study. Janice had experienced a recent death of a close family member, and they and their husbands had shared a meal together the night before. The subject came up of Rose meeting me the next day, and I guessed that Rose expressed some nervousness about it. The end result was an apparent last-minute decision to have Janice accompany her.

We sat down in a booth where Rose had been eating a salad. She sat across from me and began what seemed like a prepared speech of sorts. It turned out to be a sincere, rather long expression of her feelings and thoughts about her adoption. Much of it I had heard before in her letters and over the phone through the years. I was conscious while she was talking that I wasn't always listening to her as carefully as I could have been. I was studying her manner of speech, expressions, eyes, hair, and earnestness.

But the gist of what she was saying was pretty clear. She'd never regretted being adopted. She saw it as God's plan for her to fulfill the best path for her life. She held no grudge against me for my decision.

Although I have done some journaling intermittently throughout my life, I have not been a daily or habitual journalist. One would think that one of the most important events of my life would have managed to be elevated to the status of a worthy journaling subject. Alas, it was not, as I don't find it in the pages of my two floral hardcover journals.

I am now dipping into the recesses of my memory bank at 72, almost 73 in a few days, to put down this momentous event in a typed form.

I remember speaking to Rose and her friend, sitting across the table from me, what I remembered from her birth. I told them that I remembered nothing of the actual birth due to the medications I'd been given that assured I would have no memory of it. But I did tell them how I remembered waking up in the middle of the night. "It was dark, and I knew I had given birth. I felt my abdomen, and it was flatter." At that moment, the emotion I had felt all those years ago overwhelmed me. "I remember such a feeling, such a terrible feeling of …". For some reason, I couldn't find the word to describe that feeling, although it should have been obvious, as it apparently was to Janice.

Janice then provided the word as I felt momentarily overcome with sadness. Tears filled my eyes, and I looked away briefly in confusion. "Loss?" Janice suggested. "Yes, loss," I said.

I quickly recovered and looked at the large tote I had brought in with me. During my frantic packing the day before, I had gathered together some gifts and photos I wanted to take to Rose. Who knows, maybe this would be my one and only chance to ever meet with her in person.

I began taking out the items one by one to give or show her, and as I did, I explained the significance of each item.

"This is a doily my sister Margie crocheted. She has lung cancer and has been making them all her life, but even more so now in her remaining days. She has lots of yarn she's accumulated from all the garage sales she used to go to. Her crocheted doilies are a lasting remembrance of herself to family and friends." I did not tell her that Margie was the only family member I had told about my pregnancy at the time it happened or that Margie lived only about 30 minutes from where Rose and her parents lived when she was adopted. Maybe they'd even seen each other at a Kansas garage sale.

I held up a large framed photo collage and said, "Rose, I'd like to introduce you to your Aunt Barbara, who lives only about an hour and a half away from you. This is my husband, Glenn, and some of our grandchildren." I remember Rose seeming to be interested in that photo and saying, "So you have grandchildren?"

"And I think you would like two of my nieces, Kathy and Paula. Say 'Hi to Rose, Kathy and Paula,'" I joked.

One special gift, a porcelain plate, which I somewhat reluctantly gave her, was something that had been in my mother's family. I was reluctant because it was very special to me, and I didn't know if she would appreciate it. I'd had a love of porcelain dinnerware, teapots, plates, and dishes, especially with floral designs, for many decades. Perhaps it had been used in my mother's home as part of a dinnerware set, or it had hung on the wall as decoration as it had in the home where I grew up. It was a beautiful floral design and originated in Germany. As I handed Rose this gift and others, she accepted them with a thank you and said, "I'll take good care of them."

I suspect most were relegated to a box in a storage room, but I have no idea. I seem to recall that she indicated she liked the old things, antique things like porcelain plates and crocheted doilies. She had told me once she was a "people pleaser," and perhaps she accepted them graciously so as not to offend or disappoint me.

One thing I gave her, that perhaps she used later, was a corn bag I had made. It was a cotton covered bag filled with dried corn that could be microwaved or chilled in the freezer, then applied to painful areas of the body. I occasionally made various simple craft items to give to family and friends. My hope was that she would, in fact, use it and, in so doing, think of me.

I showed her a framed photo of my family with my parents and siblings when I was in my early fifties and still had brown hair. A professional photographer took it. Knowing she wasn't planning to tell her children or parents about our meeting, I didn't offer it. The same photo was in a spiraled book I had authored honoring my mother that I had sent to Rose at some point.

She had not reciprocated with any photos to show me, probably not wanting to form any bridge to her current life. She feared that if her children knew of her meeting with me, they'd no doubt tell their grandmother, her mother. "I really don't want to burden her or my dad with this now." She was vague with the reasons for this, but it seems perhaps they had some issues that may have been difficult related to her adoptive brother, several years younger than she. I didn't press her on this. At one point, she said, "Everyone thinks it's a bad idea that I meet with you, except me."

I remember an uncomfortable moment when Rose responded to my comment that at least if I'd never met her, perhaps we'd have met in the next life. She responded with a question frequently asked by evangelical Christians, "Are you saved?"

To a Catholic, this is a hard one. Simply declaring that Jesus is your Lord and Savior is not an assurance of redemption in the

Catholic way of thinking. It's more complicated for the Catholic Christian, and according to church doctrine, one must be saved by the Spirit plus the waters of Baptism and the forgiveness of sin through the sacrament of penance in confession. I hesitated trying to formulate an answer and felt somehow excluded from the company of the two people sitting across from me. I don't think I was able to come up with much of an answer on the spur of that moment.

Rose left the booth to go to the restroom at one point, leaving Janice and me alone. "I don't really understand her reluctance to tell her own children," I said to Janice.

"This is all so new to her," Janice said in understandable defense of her friend. I remember thinking then that perhaps this meeting was just indeed a start and that a relationship could continue to develop.

Janice spoke of some things that I have no recollection of except that I recall thinking as she was talking, "My precious time with my daughter is being taken in conversation with a stranger, and this may be the last time I ever get a chance to be with her." I had no animosity toward Janice. In fact, I liked her and felt that she seemed to understand me. Had she not been there, I would have had no good photographs of our reunion except for possible selfies. Still, I felt a sense of being cheated from my time with my daughter, not because of any malice of anyone, just the circumstances of the moment.

I had watched Rose walk away and wanted to imprint her gait and general way of moving on my memory. This I added to my collection of memories about her that formed my composite impression of her. She was slim, able to wear short boots with two-inch heels, well-fitting jeans and walked easily with a flexibility that must have been to her advantage on the tennis courts in her high school years and beyond.

Having gotten to the state finals in high school was evidence to me that perhaps she'd inherited and surpassed some of my athletic ability in tennis. It was a sport I'd played throughout my young adulthood. However, I'd never gotten past the beginning intermediate level. In any event, she was a healthy-looking, attractive 49-year-old. Her hair was still brown, curly and to her shoulders. Her brown eyes smiled when she smiled. I can't be sure as I look at her photo, but I think she has dimples, as do I.

Unlike me, though, she is sure about her religious faith. She and her friend Janice frequently interjected references to the Bible. I learned they were members of a Southern Baptist church and had both been teachers in a Christian elementary school closely aligned with Baptist teachings.

In our conversation, I learned we had different beliefs about a few social issues of the day.

I am impressed by her exemplary life in all evidence, including her Facebook posts, family life, and general good behavior. Meeting her in person only solidified that impression.

Our meeting lasted an hour and 15 minutes. Rose said she would have to leave if she was going to make it to her youngest child's sports event. "I missed many of the sports activities of my other children because I was working," she explained. "I'm determined not to miss any of my youngest child's now that I have the time."

So, our reunion that day was ending. It went by fast and was a decent enough start. We stood and hugged again. As we were still hugging, Rose said something comforting and indicated to me that she liked me, I thought, at least my physical appearance.

"You are beautiful, Judy," she said. "There's still hope for me."

I found her statement both flattering and puzzling. She was indeed a beautiful woman in my eyes and in the eyes of my family and friends who later saw her photo. I have prints to prove it from photos Janice took with my phone.

I left hoping but not knowing if there would be subsequent visits and perhaps the beginning of an ongoing relationship between us.

I continued on to the monastery in Fort Smith to join my sister Barbara and the rest of her community of nuns to join in the final goodbye for my eighth-grade teacher. Although it was a somber occasion with the traditional ceremonies to honor the deceased, inwardly I felt a sense of joy due to having just met my long-lost daughter.

I shared my good news with Barbara when I arrived and later to Glenn and other family and friends back home. I enjoyed their responses of happiness for me as well as congratulations as if I had given birth to a child. It was a rebirth of hope that I hadn't entirely lost her, despite her adoption into a new family.

My elation mellowed as the months followed with no response from Rose to a letter and poem I sent her after returning home. She didn't communicate with me in any form. I had thought perhaps a text, at least, that she had enjoyed meeting me. But then she would have possibly felt the need to add something about meeting me again, and this was not her intent I eventually learned.

None the less, I really enjoyed showing her photo to relatives and friends and asking them if they knew who this was a photo of before telling them. All remarked how much she looked like me, and that it must be Rose, my daughter.

# Letter to Rose After our Meeting

*April 3, 2018*

*Dear Rose,*

*The enclosed poem consolidates some of my thoughts since our meeting. Perhaps it's an improvement over a long letter. Personalized poetry is a hobby I've picked up this past year.*

*I find I can express myself in ways that are harder in prose. Maybe my journalism degree is paying off in a practical way — or not!*

*Also, I enclosed a print that I had an extra of. Janice did a good job as a photographer! I would love to hear from you. My email is jbock@xxxx should you wish to correspond via that avenue.*

*Prayers, peace and love,*

*Judy*

# Love-15, Her Serve

April 2018

It was a day of stormy rain

as I traveled to a burger place.

Would I find what I was looking for

when I met her face to face?


A decision made when I was young

left me sad with regret when once awake.

I had no counsel and was not informed.

I often wondered, "Was it a mistake?"


But then I came to a place agreed,

found welcome arms and smiles.

For the first time ever, I held my lovely child —

so worth the traverse of thunderous miles.


I gathered gifts I gave to her.

"They hold significance," I said.

A golden chain of infinite love, a floral plate,

a bag of corn, an intricate circle of thread.

"They look alike," so many say

when their images they behold.

A combination of nature and nurture —

I ponder these words experts foretold.


I admire the courage she must have had

to defy those who said no to our meeting.

A chance to share, if only briefly,

an hour and 15 minutes — so fleeting!


But now I feel great joy and peace

as I settle back to my life once more.

I have my memories; our photos are framed.

Now the ball is in her court — just as before.

# Shall we Meet Again?

Letter to Rose Jan. 31, 2019

*Dear Rose,*

*I hope this finds you well and happy. It was close to a year since we met at McDonald's on Feb. 23. That was such a wonderful experience.*

*I am writing to let you know I will be traveling again to your area the last week in February and am hopeful we can visit again.*

*My husband and I are attending a conference in Fort Smith from Feb. 22-24 and will be staying in Fort Smith and Fayetteville or Bentonville until March 1.*

*During that time, we plan to visit my sister Barbara at St. Scholastica Monastery, attend a Lady Tigers Mizzou basketball game with the Razorbacks in Fayetteville Feb. 28, visit sites including Crystal Bridges and, last but certainly not least, visit with you if possible.*

*The conference ends at 1 p.m. Sunday, Feb. 24, and we'll stay in Fort Smith Sunday and Monday nights, then drive to Fayetteville or Bentonville for the next three overnights.*

*I (we) would love to visit with you <u>any time</u> after the conference that would work for you, either in Fort Smith or maybe Crystal Bridges. Perhaps your husband would like to meet us as well or someone else of your choice: If you prefer it be just you and I, that is OK with me.*

*I look forward to hearing from you by phone, email or snail mail and I will be anxiously awaiting your reply.*

167

*With love,*

*Judy*

*...-...-.... cell*

*P.S. Crystal Bridges is closed on Tuesdays*

*...-...-...land judy..,..,.@......*


Note in Response from Rose Feb 6, 2019

*Dear Judy,*

*Hope you enjoy your time in Arkansas. As I stated when we met last February, I do not desire to communicate further and only wanted to meet you the one time because you wanted to. Each time you contact me, it causes me emotional grief. Please stop. I can try to understand your perspective, but please respect mine.*

*Rose*

*Do not come here (to our home.)*


I don't think I heard her loud and clear "No!" until this final rejection following my invitation for a second meeting the year following our first meeting. To me, it sounded angry. She finally got through to me. It hurt but was effective. I finally heard her. She apparently had said at our meeting that it was our one-time meeting, and I couldn't or wouldn't hear that clearly.

For a long time, I had displayed a print I'd made from her Facebook page of Rose and Richard's wedding photo she had posted publicly and another photo of Rose on my bedside table. After this emphatic refusal to meet me a second time, I put them away in a keepsake chest. I was hurting and did not need a frequent reminder of her rejection. I still kept a few photos of her and her children in my office, where I am now writing.

After this refusal, I felt a sense of finality in my hopes of ever having a continuing relationship with Rose or her family. I stopped looking at her or her children's Facebook public postings for the most part.

Per her request, I am not communicating further with letters or phone calls. The one exception was to update her on my open-heart surgery so that she could know about her own health decisions. She is going on with her life without my occasional entreaties to be part of it. I am going on with mine with no lingering hope that she will ever change her mind.

Had I known that my cards with included notes or letters caused her "emotional grief," as Rose wrote in her final brief letter, I think I would have resisted the repeated urge to change her mind somehow to meet me and to form a relationship.

# Shelter in Place

It was an unprecedented time in my lifetime, as with everyone else, when our city and much of the United States had "shelter at home" orders in early April 2020 because of Covid 19.

A lot happened in the previous several months. My open-heart surgery in January was followed by the evolving development and danger of the spread of the Corona virus that was first reported in China. Near my four-week follow-up visit to my cardiac surgeon and my cardiologist, more and more reports of sickness and deaths from the virus came on the news reports.

It still hadn't hit the United States at an alarming rate, and we continued to plan for our RV trip to Arizona. Getting the go-ahead and even encouragement from my doctors, we began our trip on March 4.

I was just at five weeks post op heart surgery and not at full energy level, nor pain-free, but mostly able to enjoy much of our trip. We visited a couple of overnights with my sister Barbara and her fellow nuns at the monastery, only an hour and a half from Rose's home. I did think of Rose as we passed one of several exits that would have led us to her home not far from the interstate, but I didn't dwell on it and honestly felt dispassionate about not having the opportunity to visit her and her family.

I believe I may have the capacity to turn off an emotional part of myself. I'd like to think that I am able to go on with my current life and focus on the positives that I am grateful for. I think that once there was finality in Rose's adamant refusal for further contact, I realized that I was fortunate to have found her happy and loved, to have been able to meet her and get a good idea of the person she was. That person is one of caring, obedience to family and religous values, loyal to her parents, protective of her children, respectful and courteous to me, sensitive, earnest and honest. I didn't pick up on a sense of humor that would have been characteristic had she been raised among my family members, but perhaps the opportunity for humor from her perspective didn't arise at our meeting.

The RV trip was challenging in the organizational aspect of preparing and serving meals within such a small kitchen, which was my main responsibility. We had brought our dog Lily and cat Rosie along with us. Actually, they are a big part of the reason for the RV in the first place, to take them with us on vacations. They added to the organizational challenge i.e. getting Lily walked at most stops and managing Rosie's litter box, to name a few.

We enjoyed much of the trip and visits with friends and family along our path but found things to be getting much more serious regarding Covid-19 on the way home. We essentially sheltered in place in our RV. We only used the restroom and ate meals in our RV. Glenn disinfected his hands or used gloves when he pumped gas.

Sheltering in place is what my former policeman cousin Phil calls "house arrest." We did leave our house for allowed activities, including working in our yard. I planted a few early vegetables in a small plot next to the house, some kale, sugar snap peas and spinach. I don't have too much hope they'll do too well because they are very old seeds, and that side of the house doesn't get too much sun. Plus, I've never had good luck getting spinach to sprout, and it was what I had on hand in my leftover seed supply to plant. Trips to the store, except for essential shopping, were to be avoided.

We started ordering groceries online for pickup service in the store's parking lot. Some learning was involved in using the store's app, but I conquered it. We generally picked up our prescriptions ourselves after donning a mask and gloves and not venturing out into the main aisles.

At home, we did the recommended hand washing for 20 seconds frequently and tried not to touch our faces, especially our noses, to avoid transmission of the unseen virus into our lungs. On days we felt a slight sore throat, one of the early symptoms, we worried we were coming down with the virus. Luckily, we did not.

We stopped using the city's hiking/biking trails. They were just too crowded, and keeping a six-foot distance from others using the trail was sometimes not easy. Bicyclists would breeze by only a couple of feet away. One rider even spit close to Glenn.

Our walking changed to the neighborhood sidewalks and streets. Sometimes we'd text one of our neighbors who lived near us, asking her if she'd like to join us on a walk six feet apart. We would each have a chance to have a lively conversation and decrease our isolation.

Another venture outdoors required a trip in the car to the Katy Trail near the Missouri River, where we checked on an eagle nest to see how things were going with new nestlings. Lily, our dog, got better at riding in the car and graduated to riding by herself in the back seat rather than on my lap, where she had been whimpering much of the way.

So, life like we never knew it, went on day after day, filled with household tasks and hobbies for which we then had seemingly endless time. I thought of Rose occasionally, but the pain and yearning had decreased significantly since our meeting and despite her refusal to meet again.

# Duty-bound and Morally Obligated

From the tone of her letter of February 2019 in response to my letter in late January suggesting a repeat meeting, I had no intention of contacting her again. I didn't intend even to tell her about my bypass surgery.

However, after being asked by my friend Cindy and another friend in the adoption search community as to my plans to tell her, I changed my mind. She had a right to know in order to make her own health decisions.

This year I didn't send her a birthday card out of consideration that communications from me caused her emotional pain. Following her birthday, I wrote a draft and had Glenn read it. He suggested some changes to make it less personal with just the facts.

This is the letter I sent:

*April 15, 2020*

*Hello Rose,*

*I am writing with some important medical information that I feel duty-bound and morally obligated to send you. I do hope it doesn't cause you emotional distress.*

*I had a triple coronary artery bypass in January and had an uneventful recovery. Others in my family with cardiovascular disease:*

*My mother — has congestive heart disease and hypertension. My Father — has strokes, aneurysms, pacemaker*

*Brother Jim — pacemaker*

*Brother Maurice — pacemaker, stroke*

*Brother Gerald — died at age 72 sudden heart attack*

*I hope this helps you with lifestyle choices and health decisions and that you and your family are well and happy.*

*Sincerely, Judy Bock*


I did not expect to hear from her, but I did wonder how she felt when she read it. Before opening it, she probably thought it was a belated birthday card and might have been angry when she saw the return address. Perhaps she was less so when she read it. During a previous conversation, either at our actual meeting or by phone, I recall her saying that she was glad she was adopted because when she went to a doctor's appointment, she didn't need to fill out the family history. This puzzled me when I thought about it later because I had sent her my family's medical history long before that conversation.

She did not acknowledge receiving this information but only mentioned in her final letter, in which she asked I not contact her further, that each time she received something from me, in her words, "caused emotional pain" for her. I surmised this was evidence of at least some conflict within herself of both wanting to have some sort of relationship with me and not wanting to rock the boat of her stable adoptive family life.

I didn't expect her to have what seemed to me a kind of unconcern about her biological health history. Perhaps this letter would give her reason not to neglect this aspect of her health.

Another vague and disturbing thought crossed my mind briefly. Had she not received previous mailings detailing her family health history and national ancestry? Perhaps they'd been lost in the mail, or the dog ate the letter; who knows? She might have skimmed the information so quickly that none of it sank in, and it was stored away or destroyed, not to be looked at again.

# Final Thoughts

One of the things recommended by people in the adoption community, including birth mothers and adoptees who write about adoption aftermath, is for the birth parent to tell the adoptee that you are sorry you gave them up.

In one of my letters, I did this. "I am happy that you had such great parents and that your family life turned out so great. For you, I am not sorry," I wrote. "But for myself, I am sorry I gave away something so precious, my flesh and blood, my own child." I have many regrets that emerged through the years once I stopped believing my mantra, "I did the right thing."

Another of my regrets was the precipitous, nearly loveless marriage I entered nine months after giving birth. It was to a college boy I dated only a short time prior to getting engaged. As I previously explained, I am convinced this was an unconscious effort to quickly get involved in thinking about something other than the loss I had just suffered and needed to forget. I needed to convince myself I had done the right thing and could just get on with my life.

For a time, the strategy to get my mind off my child's loss worked well. Planning a wedding and adjusting to a new husband certainly did occupy me. It was the sure escape from thinking about Rose. I was in denial. I would not admit to the loss as something of huge proportions that would surely affect the rest of my life. After all, I had done the right and proper thing and provided my child with a family through trusted sources.

I am sorry now and feel an apology is in order to the young man and his family, who I selfishly snared into my strategy of emotional survival.

I was sorry for myself when I was unsuccessful in getting pregnant again in later years, all the time knowing I had given away my baby to strangers I had never even met. I will never know how a different script, that of keeping her, may have turned out for both of us.

But recently, I realized I have made an important shift in my thinking and possibly an improvement in my mental and emotional well-being. So, if no one ever reads this, it has at least this benefit.

That shift is the following. Knowing that things are not going to progress in my efforts to build a relationship with my lost daughter, I consciously realize that I am free now to put my eggs in the basket of my existing life with the family that is available to me. Part of this family is the stepchildren I have probably never bonded with as much as I could have, and also to the grandchildren I have acquired through my present (and God help me, last) marriage.

I have told others that I have step-children and grandchildren, the distinctive change now being that I don't usually put "step" in front of "my grandchildren" and sometimes not in front of "my children" during conversations. I feel like a true grandma to these children who are a part of my life now. Others with stepchildren tell me that they totally understand. The children occasionally call me mom and introduce me to others that way, but all the grandkids call me grandma. In a way, I feel released from a burden of sorts, that is, from the intermittent but continuing effort to establish a relationship with my lost child. This memoir has continued to be part of my effort with its healing and reopening of old wounds.

As I think of my life now and of the daughter I gave away to strangers, I feel immensely fortunate and grateful that I had the opportunity to finally meet her.

*My husband Glenn poses with some of our grandchildren at his retirement party in 2019.*

So to Rose, should you ever read this, I wish to thank you for this truly selfless gift you gave to me. I wish we could have continued a relationship, but this is apparently best for you. After all, that's what adoption is supposed to accomplish, isn't it, to do what's best for the child? Your adoptive parents were the big winners in getting you. The fact that birth parents are left with grief or regret to a greater or lesser degree is regrettable but secondary.

Writing this memoir was a struggle for me. I never looked forward to getting on my computer to dredge up memories that upset me. As I said in another place, this was a project I felt called to do, something of a pilgrimage and a duty. I hope it benefits someone, especially expectant parents considering the adoption option and sheds light on the struggles that beset those who do.

*Author poses with her dog Lily while resting along a trail in Florida in 2022*

# Appendix

## More Communications With my Daughter

Occasionally I would write a letter to my unknown daughter just to make some sort of connection and to put on paper some thoughts and feelings.

Here is one of the first.

*September 24, 1981*

*Dear Child,*

*I don't know your name — I had called you Jody and only recently learned that you are a female, although I had always thought so due to your low birth weight — more typical of girl babies. I was never told your sex and at the time of your birth I didn't insist on knowing or even seeing you or holding you as I now very much wish I had. At the time of your birth my doctor recommended that I know very little about you except that you were healthy and weighted 5 # 15 oz. I believed in his, what I thought was superior wisdom at the time, and went along with the belief that the less I knew the better for me, and that I would be able to forget about you in time. I have never been able to totally forget that I gave birth to you.*

*My pregnancy with you was very uneventful. I worked for about the first seven months and did my best to eat well during the pregnancy. I remember you moving around inside of me and I would enjoy this and being able to feel you thrust your leg or arm against my abdomen. I was unable to tell my own family except for one sister about my pregnancy, due to shame and guilt for not having been married to your birth father and fear that it would be too upsetting to my parents. I have recently told another sister and will someday, I*

180

*think, inform my other brothers and sisters. I am still very hesitant to tell my parents for fear the benefits would not outweigh the possible negative results — they are in their mid-seventies.*

*At the time you were born it was not as common as it became later or socially acceptable for unmarried mothers to keep their babies. I was hopeful that you would have a better life and greater chances of happiness with a mother and a father who could provide you with a good home. I could not provide you a father, nor did I consider it feasible financially or socially to keep you as a single parent. I was told your adoptive parents were good Christian people and that your adoptive mother resembled me in physical appearance. (Years later when I told this to Rose Diane she said this was totally untrue. Her mother was short statured and looked nothing like me, she said.) It was the most painful emotional experience I have ever had — to surrender you for adoption. I wanted you very much and knew you must have been a beautiful baby.*

*You would most likely appreciate knowing some of your genetic heritage and family medical history. I will attempt to tell you some of the facts about myself and what I remember of your father whom I haven't seen in years.*

*I am from a large family, three brothers and four sisters and grew up in a small town called Pilot Grove, Missouri. My family is Roman Catholic, and my parents at this writing still are alive and in good health living in Pilot Grove. My father needed a pacemaker several years ago and my mother is being treated for high blood pressure, but otherwise is healthy. My father had three sisters and four brothers and he grew up near and lived most of his life in Pilot Grove.*

*His grandparents came to this country from Germany in the 1800's and among other things homesteaded land in Kansas. My mother also comes from a large family by the name of Schuster. Her father came from Germany with his parents when he was a boy and settled in Missouri. So I am all German as you can deduce.*

*Both my mother and father have sisters who had breast cancer. My mother's youngest sister recently died of cancer. My own brothers and sisters are all well with no chronic medical diseases. My oldest sister has had more than her share of emotional problems for which she presently is receiving psychiatric care. There is no history of diabetes or kidney disease on either side of my family. My father's parents lived to an old age. My mother's father died of a stroke when she was six. Her mother died of old age. (She also had a stroke I think, prior to her death.)*

*I had recently graduated from nurse's training when I became pregnant with you. Your birth father and I had met when he worked as an orderly in St. John's Hospital in Springfield, Missouri, where I was a student. He was working his way through Southwest Missouri State College with a goal of getting a degree in history. He was a very handsome, popular, and energetic person, but not ready for family responsibilities. Unfortunately our relationship was not strong enough to build a marriage on. His family name was xxxxxx, and he grew up near Springfield, Missouri. I know very little about his family except that he had at least two brothers in Springfield. My last information is that your birth father, Josh, lived in Springfield and was divorced.*

*I went to live with a very close friend, Diane Welch, in Tulsa, Oklahoma, after my pregnancy was confirmed. She helped me very much. One of my sisters, Margie, also gave me support. After your birth I was very depressed, and in trying to forget about it and to replace (unsuccessfully) the loss I felt, I rushed into a marriage with the first person I dated after the pregnancy. We moved from Tulsa to*

*Chicago where we separated and divorced after four and one half years of a rather unhappy marriage. I have since married a wonderful man and moved to the country near Blue Mounds, Wisconsin. My husband knows that I had a baby years ago. We have no children yet, but have been trying for several years.*

*I feel that I need to tell you more about myself. I am still in nursing, but am not totally happy with it as a career. I am most happy when I am gardening. I also took up beekeeping last year and have two hives. My family on both sides are from agrarian backgrounds. I enjoy original art, music, baking and crafts. It is a goal of mine to go back to college, but I have no definite career goal in mind. I'd love to have a greenhouse someday. Mostly I'd like a family with children in it. I believe in Christian values, but am open to many different points of view. I am not a strict Catholic, but I do attend church.*

*I hope this information is helpful to you and that it will help you know more of where you came from and that you understand you were very much wanted.*

*I would expect that you would possibly feel anger towards me for not keeping you. In a way I feel you are justified, but I hope you can forgive me.*

*I pray that you have a good family with your adoptive parents. Many children don't get along with their parents at various points in their life. I was never very close to mine after early childhood and it wasn't until I was into my late twenties that I learned to truly love them and accept them as they were.*

*There is so much to say, but I have, I think, covered the main points. If you ever wish to contact me for any reason — to obtain more of your background or whatever — I would be willing to communicate with you further. I don't know under what circumstance you will, if ever, read this, but I wanted something to have available in case you searched for me. I hope to give one copy to my sister Berniece and one I will inform my husband to be filed in a safe place in case something happens to me.*

*I have felt it best not to attempt a search for you until you are older — I hope this is the best decision — however I may change my mind.*

*You are the only child I may ever have by birth. I am so sorry I wasn't a stronger, more assertive person, who was able to be a single parent for you. It is my hope and prayer that we could someday meet. I hope also your parents would not feel threatened that they will lose you by your contacting and possibly getting to know me or your birth father.*

*My love to you,*

*Judy Bock Camera*

I do not know if Rose ever read this or subsequent letters I wrote to her through the years. I sent her letters that I had written through the years along with documents, related to my search for her, to her home years after initially contacting her.

*April 7, 1982*

*Dear Jody,* (This was a temporary name I gave my daughter.)

*I'm writing this letter on your 13th birthday. I haven't forgotten you, nor have I stopped wondering about you.*

*I wonder what you look like. I imagine you are very pretty with brown eyes and dark hair. I imagine you are sensitive and fun loving.*

*I hope and pray you are happy and that you love and are loved by your parents.*

*I'm so sorry I couldn't be your parent. Someday I hope to have the opportunity to talk to you about that. I very much regret that I am not your parent, but I can't change what has been done long ago. I can only act in the present.*

*I have been trying for some time now to locate your parents to let them know I'm wondering about you and that I am available to you or them if either of you want any information from me. I suspect they are afraid and possibly angry about my coming into your lives again.*

*Jody, I have suffered much emotional pain as a result of surrendering you for adoption. The loss I felt was almost unbearable. I was severely depressed after your birth and mistakenly tried to replace your loss by quickly marrying a man I didn't really care about. That marriage ended and was soon replaced by a marriage to a man I loved very much. We tried desperately to have children without success. Because of my loss of you, I had an abnormal need to have children. This put a terrible strain on my 2nd marriage and along with other factors including my husband's inability to cope or unwillingness to, caused the breakdown in our relationship and eventual ending of the marriage. At this time I have been separated from him for almost 3 months.*

*I hope your adoption has not been a problem for you. I hope your parents have been able to fill in some gaps about me and that you get answers if you have questions about your history or mine. I hope to get information from your birth father about his family for you. I knew him my senior year in nursing school. He was very handsome, fun loving, energetic and popular. He was working his way through college with a major in history. I think he had a serious drinking problem, but it did not interfere with his job or school that I was aware of. I did not care enough for him nor feel he was responsible enough to marry. In hindsight he would have been preferable to my first husband.*

*I have been working as a nurse since 1968. I enjoy many sports including tennis and skiing. I like nature and gardening. I've considered changing careers to horticulture, but have recently decided against that. I would like us to get to know each other someday and to have at least a friendly relationship.*

*I pray you can forgive me, although I have had a hard time forgiving myself for letting you go.*

*With my love, your birth mother, Judy*

Letter to Rose Diane dated January 27, 1983

*Dear Jody,*

*I have decided to call you Jody which is what I occasionally called you near the time of your birth. It is a combination of my name and your father's. had I been able to keep you I would have chosen a more "Catholic" name after a saint such as Christin which actually is a derivation of Christ — the number one saint. You are number one to me even though I don't know you and may never have the opportunity.*

*Sometimes I'm very sad when I think about what I have missed and am missing by not being your parent. I hope not to spend a lot of time thinking about that because it really won't help me or you. One thing I can do now is from time to time write a letter to you to let you know what I'm thinking as we both grow older.*

*One Of the things I did want to tell you is I feel some sort of bond with you even now. I remember when I was your age that I felt very alone and isolated and really didn't think I had a friend in the world. I hope somehow you know that I am your friend if you ever feel that way. I hope that through time and miles you are feeling that bond and that caring I send out to you.*

*I realize Jody that you may not at all be interested in any emotional sharing from me.*

*Please forgive me for this.*

*Remember I love you anyway. There I go again. Just a hopeless sentimentalist.*

*Bye for now, Judy*

I believe these letters to my daughter served the purpose of venting my emotions. Whether the writing of them lifted my mood or lessened my sadness is certainly debatable. I would suppose that many people would say I was still wallowing in my misery. Kinder hearts might say I was just trying to process the trauma.

*April 10, 1984*

*Dear Jody,*

*Please excuse this stationery. It's about all I could find at the moment. I have some spare time so thought I'd use it to write you a letter.*

*Well, our birthdays have come and gone again. Maybe I've never told you yours is a day before mine. The day after you were born my friend Diane and her family brought me birthday gifts. I wasn't in a very happy mood to say the least. Dr. Maddox had me on some sort of antidepressant or tranquilizer — I can't remember what exactly. I think it would have helped me more if he had sent someone to talk to me.*

*I was too ignorant and unaware in general of my own needs at the time. I just felt the pain of losing you, and it didn't seem like there was any alternative. I didn't think of one and no one suggested one.*

*I often wonder if I had seen you, held you etc. would I have been able to part with you. Would I have gotten the courage to try to keep you? Anyway, what's done is done — I missed my chance to be your parent. I only pray you've had good ones.*

*I wonder if I'll ever find you and meet you. There are things I want to tell you. I expect it to be a difficult time from what other birth parents have experienced after reunions. A fuller realization of what they have lost is brought into clearer focus. What will be a second loss will be a rejection by you.*

*Some adoptees want nothing to do with their birth parents. I suspect that might be out of loyalty for their adoptive parents, or fear of the unknown. I am praying you are a loving enough person to be able to share a little of yourself if only briefly with the person who gave you birth. I hope you have more courage than I did, not to reject someone who could be the best thing that ever happened to you, because of family or other societal pressures and fears. That's how I see my loss of you. I didn't know you — so I can't say I rejected you. I'm sure if I had seen you I would have fallen in love totally.*

*It may not be good for me to think of you too much if there is nothing I can do to correct the situation that continues to be a burden for me. I think though that it helps me to get some of my feelings down and maybe someday you will understand me and know me better by reading things I have written. I hope to continue to be active in the adoption reform movement and to speak out and write about the birth parent perspective. These efforts at trying to change what I feel is abuse of birth parents as well as their children make me feel better.*

*Doing nothing is not right, and I feel guilty if I don't keep working at it. Searching for you is another thing that makes me feel I'm doing something positive.*

*I will soon be marrying again. I am somewhat anxious about it, but feel hopeful it will be good for me. Tom is so stable, and that's one thing I hope to get from him. I pray I'll be able to give also. He is a very good man, a good companion, very intelligent, warm and he loves me very much. I worry I'll never be able to love him as much as he loves me, but he seems quite satisfied with what he's able to feel from me so far. I have often theorized that my loss of you was a big reason for my marital instability. I know it has played a big part. Tom wants me to find you and is very interested in this issue in my life.*

*Well Jody, I'll sign off for a while. I hope you are having a good life. Somehow I feel you are. I'm looking forward to meeting you someday. Please give me a chance if only for a one time meeting.*

*Sincerely,*

*And with love Judy Bock*

Notebook Notes from Phone Call to Rose April 2, 1991

I had called directory assistance in the city where I learned Rose was attending college to see if she was listed in the phone book. Sure enough she was. I wrote out some things I would ask her if I managed to get her on the line and some expected responses.

Here is the script with questions and expected answers that I used to help with the call. I wrote down some of her actual responses, and they are only a few in quotes, but I don't know how close to the script our phone conversation actually was.

*Is Rose there?*

*Yes, this is Rose.*

*I'm not sure if I have the right person. Is your BD April 7, 69?*

*Yes*

*Rose, is now a good time for you: I would like to talk with you for a few minutes. Yes. Who is this?*

*This is Judy Bock, your birth mother.*

*I received your mother's letter 3 yrs ago and your note.*

*I understand your concerns. I'm not asking anything of you, I just want to know how you are and to let you know I still am thinking about you.*

*I don't know if this is good to be calling you or not, but I'm afraid of losing track of you. Are you upset with my calling?*

*It sounds like you have a wonderful family — it's what I hoped for you. What is your major? "elementary ed, I'm a senior"*

*Melia (She is my great niece who is adopted) — can see the love she gets and am comforted that you got the same. She was showered with love and attention. Her parents were also open with her about her adoption and birth parents as much as she was interested in.* I had this in my notes as a possible topic of phone conversation.

*"I am engaged to Richard ..... He's a computer major at the University of Arkansas."*

*There is another Judy Bock in my city, should you ever try to look me up. My middle name is Ellen, so that should differentiate us.*

*Soundex* (I told her I was registered in the International Soundex Reunion Registry, a well-respected organization that facilitated the exchange of information between adoptees and birth families.)

*Am open to further contact*

*Tennis*

*Happy BD*

*Would you mind dropping me a line every year or so?*

My memory of this call is not really clear. I wish I had written more down on my script sheet or entered notes into a journal. I do remember that she seemed fairly open to hearing from me. Notably, she was comfortable letting me know she would be getting married and to whom. This was crucial in learning her future married name.

It was this call or a subsequent one that Rose told me, "I think God was preparing me for your call. I just watched a TV show about adoption and reunions just a couple days ago."


Letter to Rose Jan 27, 2004

*Dear Rose,*

*How are you and your family?*

*I completed a memoir of my mother, and I thought you might find it interesting. it will give you a glimpse into the personality of my family and your biological roots.*

*I hope you enjoy it. It was fun putting together.*

*We have been busy here at our house. We took full-time care of three of our grandkids ages 5, 3 and 1 last week. They were a handful, but taking the oldest, a girl, to kindergarten and the two boys to daycare really helped. I enjoyed them much of the time, especially the baby. I'm not their blood grandma, but they call me grandma.*

*I hope things have settled down some for you. I sure appreciated your letter at Christmas and the photo of your sweet children.*

*How is Richard's father, and are you OK since your surgery? Call, write or email when you can.*

*Sincerely, Judy*


Email from Rose May 31, 2004 8:58 p.m.

*Dear Judy,*

*Sorry I have not been able to write back to you. We are still going through some pretty stressful times at our home right now. I still am not ready to go any further with our relationship at this point. I am only comfortable with e-mail or letter writing for now. We have had a very rough year and will continue to be emotionally and physically drained for the next several months due to circumstances out of my control. I can't go into details, but please understand that I just cannot handle anything else on my plate right now. It is stressful for me to even find the time to turn on the computer.*

*Thanks for being patient, Rose*

(I responded that day by email.)

*From: Judy Bock*

*To: Rose ...*

*Sent: Tuesday, June 01, 2004 12:52 PM*

*Dear Rose,*

*Thanks for letting me know of your current situation. I'm sorry you are having a stressful time, however it is said that this is the way God shapes us to fulfill our purpose here and to purify us.* (Apparently I felt the need to offer something of a religious nature, thinking she would be accepting and receptive. As I read it now, I'm not so sure this would have been helpful.)

*I'll put you and your family on my prayer list so that you may come through your stress with renewed strength and peace.*

*I understand why you don't want to overload yourself. I will continue to be patient and trust you will go forward when the time is right for you. Sometimes I wonder myself if I am ready for such a major event in my life. Most of the time I say yes. But I am not ready if you aren't, as I want you to want it as much as I do.*

*My life has been pretty full of family activities and responsibilities. My mother is failing and we don't expect her to be with us too much longer. She is 94 now and we eight kids are still taking turns caring for her at her home in Pilot Grove, Mo.*

*Our family here in Harrisburg has been busy helping out with my husband's oldest son's three children, ages six, four and 18 months. They are now with their daddy in Kentucky. We hope he can keep them, as their mother is very unstable.*

*I have the photo you sent at Christmas framed and in my home office. I pray for your children when I look at it. They are beautiful.*

*I wish there was more I could do to help you with your stress, but this is about all I have to offer now.*

*Here is a scripture verse I picked out for you:*

*Then the Lord will guide you always and give you plenty even on the parched land.*

*He will renew your strength, and you shall be like a watered garden, like a spring whose water never fails.*

*Isaiah 58:11*

Again, I am somewhat struck with my religious reference here, as I don't generally appreciate other people doing this. I had been going to a Bible study at my church, and perhaps this was a natural outcome. Also, as I had mentioned earlier, I thought Rose would be receptive and think well of me for this.

Letter to Rose *October 21, 2005*

*Dear Rose,*

*I hope this letter finds you and your family in good health and happiness.*

*It was good to talk to you in July. I am sending you a book, Birthbond: Reunions Between Birth Parents and Adoptees, that I recently reread. I encourage you to read it or at least parts of it in preparation for a meeting that I pray we might have in the not too distant future.*

*I understand some of your difficulty in discussing this subject with your parents.*

*Ironically, it was a similar reluctance to share the fact of my pregnancy with my parents that led me in part to place you in an adoptive family and to keep it a secret from most of my family until years later.*

*It may be especially helpful to you in proceeding towards our reunion if you read chapter 12 in Birthbond, which is "Post-Reunion and the Adoptive Parents."*

*If you haven't yet talked to your parents about a reunion, I've enclosed a copy of a chapter from Lost and Found: The Adoption Experience by B.J. Lifton, a professional writer and birth mother. The chapter's title is "Telling the Adoptive Parents."*

*With all this, perhaps you will be able to discuss this with your parents and anyone else in your family with more comfort and be ready for us to meet.*

*Would this spring be too early for you? Spring break for my husband's daughter, Melissa, is March 18-26, 2006. she will be going on her senior trip and this would be a good time for Glenn and me to get away.*

*We could meet you wherever you would like within driving distance for us — Eureka Springs perhaps. I envision Thorncrown chapel near Eureka Springs as a special place befitting a reunion such as ours. You may have another suggestion.*

*I want to meet you alone first, perhaps spend a couple of hours together or so and then later we could include our husbands, your children or whomever you would like to have with you.*

*I've been thinking and praying about this since our July phone call in between the busy happenings of my life. I believe God has guided me to this point and to this invitation to you, and I trust He will guide you as well.*

*With hope and affection, Judy*

Well, I believe this must have been a bit much, to say the least. Much too zealous on my part. Her response confirmed this.

Despite my persistence over the years and entreaties to have a reunion, Rose gave only an occasional indication she shared my desire to meet or continue a dialogue. One letter seemed to have a glimmer of hope, (or did I read that into it?) when she said, "I am **not yet** ready to meet you face to face." I of course interpreted the "not yet" to mean that she might be ready at some future date.

As I look back now, I must have been an annoying presence in her life, begging for something she could not be comfortable with, not then, nor in the future.

I kept hearing about all the wonderful reunions that were often initiated by the adoptee. These adoptees had longed for information about their birth mother in particular and wanted to know why she had placed them for adoption. Reunions, even one-time meetings, seemed to satisfy some need deep inside the adoptee's psyche that put together the missing pieces of their identities.

Apparently, Rose didn't have this need. Not fully realizing this, I sent her the book described in the letter with it that contained personal accounts of adoptees, birth family members and adoptive parents who attested to their need and understanding of reunions. Rose returned the book with the following letter. The underlines and parentheses are hers.

*Letter from Rose November 2, 2005*

*Dear Judy,*

*Thank you for the invitation to meet you and for the book on reunions. With all the various sports and activities each of the children are involved in, I haven't had much time to sit down and write back. I did read over the book, but I couldn't relate to the same point of view as the authors.*

*I have never had a desire (as those in the book did as adopted children) to seek out my birth parents. I have always known I was adopted. There were never any secrets. I also never felt the <u>loneliness</u> (mentioned in the book) or as if some part of me was missing due to the fact I was adopted. I have always felt secure and loved, and that my life was as God intended. In His sovereignty, He placed me where I was supposed to be and I've never questioned it.*

*However, I <u>have</u> been curious about what you and my birth father looked like, as well as what nationality I am (German, Polish, Italian, French, or what?)*

*Besides that, I've never really wanted to know more, nor have I ever had the desire to seek out my biological parents. I am content with things as they are and do not need to meet.*

*I do not regret talking to you or receiving your letters. I did talk more with my parents about you, and they were actually fine with whatever I needed to do.*

*If I were you, I would probably want to meet a child I had given birth to. So I don't blame you for wanting to meet me. But from my perspective, I have no desire to meet. I'm sorry for the hurt and disappointment this decision causes you, but I will pray for you that God will fill the void in your heart that was caused by giving me up for adoption.*

*I'm returning your book having read through most of it and not relating to it, so I thought you might want it back.*

*Again, I will keep you in my prayers.*

*Sincerely, Rose*

So that seemed pretty clear, at least to most average readers I would think, but not to me who had blinders on and could not accept the finality of her words. I was disappointed and somewhat hurt by her return of the book and what she said about not relating to adoptees that needed reunions.

Even now I am puzzled about her comment that she didn't know her nationality. I had emphasized in interviews by the prospective adoptive parents' lawyer prior to her birth, at least I thought I did, that I was 100% German. I didn't know Josh's ancestry, so I hadn't offered that. I knew very little about Josh's family other than he had a couple of brothers and was from a small town not far from my nursing school and the hospital where we met.

Whether I told Rose of my heritage prior to this letter I don't recall.

Letter to Rose *March 26, 2015*

*Dear Rose,*

*Again I write as your birthday approaches. This may be the last letter you will receive from me, which I will explain in the following paragraphs.*

*I plan in the near future to send you a journal I've written since 1983, letters to you. In a separate mailing, you should receive a large scrapbook. It includes documents of my family history, search papers, photos, writings and more letters. So many words, so much repetition, perhaps overwhelming in volume and content.*

*A word I meditated on this morning in my spiritual reading was in fact the word, "words". I thought about how they are symbols of thoughts, feelings, facts, with power to unite, divide, inspire, inform and so on.*

*My sister's theory is that I've given you too much information, so that you have no need or desire to meet me because you already have everything about me that you could ever want.*

*Certainly the volume of what I've communicated to you in the past plus now what I will send in the days ahead may give justification to her theory. I would like to believe that words and photos (which speak even more volumes) are no substitute for the real flesh and blood and emotional coming together in real life.*

*I sincerely hope and pray that the abundance of words hasn't burdened you in any way, and I apologize if this is the case. Know that it mostly ends here with this letter and the packages. I said "mostly" because I may not be able to refrain from sending you a birthday card in later years, possibly with a short note. I promise — a short note, maybe only a signature.*

*I end with these words: I love you. I want the best for you. If your adoption was in the Creator's plan so that you could achieve your best path, I accept it and honor it. I am thankful you went to superlative parents. I now set you free of expectations, obligations, responsibilities of any kind in regard to me. Someday, if you choose, we will say hello. But for now, goodbye, Rose. May you live in peace and happiness.*

*Judy*

Rose's response *April 2, 2015*

*Dear Judy,*

*In response to your letter, there is nothing you could have said or not said that had anything to do with us meeting or not. It is out of honor to my parents who raised me. Hope you can understand. I hold no ill will toward you and never have. I do feel this is God's plan.*

*With love and peace, Rose*

The short note was on a sheet of whimsical stationery with illustrations of three cartoon sheep in a hot air balloon in the top corner and a smiling rising sun in the bottom opposite corner. A quote from the Bible reads: The Lord's love never ends. His mercies never stop. They are new every morning. LAMENTATIONS 3:22, 13

This is not the first time she stated that she was protecting her parents by not meeting me or having an ongoing relationship.

Looking back at my persistence after numerous rejections and refusals, I feel I was definitely a pest and a thorn in Rose's side. She verified this in one of her last notes that every time she got a letter from me it brought up emotional turmoil and sometimes questions from her children that caused her discomfort. I regret and am saddened to have caused this in her life. I now sometimes wonder if I should have backed off long ago after the first or second rejections. On the other hand, had I not been persistent, I might not have ever met her.

# Articles I Wrote

I would, from time to time, write pieces related to my experience as a birth mother for a class I was taking or to try to get published. The following article titled, "Infertility and the Birth Parent," is not dated. It was not published anywhere.

### *Infertility and the Birth Parent*

*By Judy E. Bock*

*I can't ever remember not wanting children. Like the majority of little girls growing up in the fifties, I was largely programmed into a goal of wife and mother. I had fantasies of being a dancer or a teacher, but what I truly wanted was to be a mother of a large brood of children. I imagined a happy, warm, bustling home filled with laughter and smells of cookies in the oven.*

*My life would be full, and I would be very happy with my children and husband.*

*I was from a large family, the youngest of eight children, and my happiest memories were of my carefree, secure childhood in the small Missouri town where my parents had settled and established firm roots. Family was the very reason, the fabric of life to me. The world outside the family had its place but was of secondary importance.*

*Perhaps it was a premonition of my fate, for I remember in my late teens expressing a fear to a close friend that I would have great difficulty having children, the one thing I had always wanted.*

*Becoming engaged during my second year of nursing school, I began my first intimate relationship with a man. We broke up, and later I became involved with a good looking college playboy type who provided some of the social life I felt I missed by going to boarding school during my high school years. In return, I provided the intimacy he needed, and as fate and inadequate birth control would have it, I became pregnant shortly after graduating from nursing school. At the time, marriage seemed very much out of the question for a number of reasons.*

*When I realized I didn't have a father for my child and a husband to help me, coupled with the shame I felt in view of my family and the small town I came from, I decided to surrender the baby to adoption. I hoped both the child and I would be better off this way.*

*My pregnancy, delivery and post-natal period seem like a bad dream now. I never saw the baby and was told it was healthy and weighed five pounds and fifteen ounces. My doctor told me it was best that I didn't know the sex of the child, and seeing the baby was not even discussed, nor did I know I had the right to see her or have more information. I went along passively, compliantly, and grief stricken. I cried during much of my hospital stay and long after I went home. My friends were very supportive, but I was inconsolable. I had gone to live away from my family and kept it a secret except to one of my sisters.*

*A private adoption was arranged through my doctor and lawyer to a couple I never met and never asked much about. I was told the woman looked a lot like me and that they were very fine people who would raise the child as a Christian. It seems tragic to me now that I placed my child into the hands of strangers who I knew so little about.*

*My method of filling in the loss I felt, was to quickly find a man to marry and have a baby I could keep. Soon after the delivery, I started dating a coworker, and we married nine months later. The marriage, unfortunately, was not good on almost any level. I briefly tried to get* pregnant but decided against it because I questioned my husband's desirability as a father and the soundness of our marriage. The marriage ended after four and one half years.

I quickly fell in love with an intense, fascinating man who I believed would make a good father. We married two years following my divorce, and after about two years of marriage, we decided it was time to start a family. We tried for a few months expecting instant results, and nothing happened. I kept getting my periods. We read articles about conceiving a child, about positions that were best and so on. Still no luck. Everyone around me was getting pregnant, including one of my best friends. My sister got married and was pregnant after one month. We kept trying — still no success. My gynecologist suggested an infertility workup with a specialist at the University Medical Center. It was shortly after this as I recall that my period was late. We were ecstatic! At last, after what seemed like an eternity — probably a year, we were going to have a baby.

We could hardly wait until the test to prove our hopes were true. I took the urine sample in and later that day called in for the results. The test was negative. I went from elation to bitter disappointment. I soon began a heavy vaginal flow that lasted over a week and continued with a light flow. Shortly thereafter, I had abdominal pain that continued for several hours and was nearly incapacitating. I saw an internist for the pain and was quickly referred to a gynecologist that day.

He examined me and suggested I get another pregnancy test. I did this, and it was positive, to my shock and renewed delight. But why the continued bleeding, and why has the pain now subsided?

Later I had an ultrasound test which showed no fetus but indicated a need for surgery due to what was a suspected incomplete miscarriage or a tubal pregnancy. Surgery lasted four hours while my husband anxiously waited outside. A tubal pregnancy was the cause of my problems. Knowing the importance of maintaining my fertility, my doctor did very tedious, painstaking microsurgery to rebuild the fallopian tube after removing the nonviable fetus. During the surgery, he had examined my other fallopian tube and concluded it was incapable of carrying an egg from the ovary, so saving the tube with the pregnancy was crucial to my continued fertility.

Instead of being terribly depressed about my tubal pregnancy, I found myself more hopeful that my husband and I could achieve a viable pregnancy. I was ready and willing to keep trying with even more determination. After I fully recovered from this surgery, my husband and I underwent a series of fertility tests which were sometimes painful and generally far from pleasant.

I kept a temperature chart and plotted carefully on a calendar the times during the month that conception could occur. My husband's sperm tests were sometimes below normal, but the last one was normal. There was a strong suspicion that some of the specimens were improperly handled, and we assumed that this caused sperm death and the resultant low count.

We took a series of antibiotics to combat a symptomless genital infection apparently common to some couples and which is thought to interfere with conception. All other tests and exams were normal.

I began to get severely depressed after starting each period. I was unaware that our unsuccessful efforts at trying to conceive were having serious negative effects on our marital relationship. My husband was afraid to tell me he no longer wanted to keep trying to have children because he knew how important it was to me.

*I don't remember at what point in this series of events I began to think more about the baby I had surrendered to adoption. It started when I read a magazine article about a birth mother who searched for and found her twins she had given up when she was 16. The article gave the address of Concerned United Birth Parents (CUB), the birth parent support group I later joined. Through CUB's newsletter, correspondence and contact with other birth mothers, and much reading of articles and books about the adoption issue, I became increasingly aware of my need to deal with this unresolved area in my life.*

*At the same time, I was struggling with my infertility. As I was awakening to and reaching a new understanding of the experience of being a birth parent, I also became increasingly more desperate to become pregnant.*

*In hindsight, I think I felt that if I couldn't have another baby, then I would know I had made a terrible mistake in giving up the only child I might ever have. I didn't want to admit that, but finally, I realized it was a terrible mistake for me to have surrendered, and I wanted desperately to believe it was a good decision. I can only pray it was not a mistake for my daughter.*

*Since it was a private adoption, I have no agency to go back to for information about her subsequent life or even her death. Despite the fact that I never saw her or held her, I feel some sort of bond and always a longing to know about her.*

*My husband and I had different perceptions of the deterioration of our marriage. He focused on the continued efforts at conception without success and how he felt I only wanted him for the purpose of conceiving a child. My perception is that many other factors were involved and that I was trying to and would eventually accept our inability to have children. We had considered adoption and were on the waiting lists at two agencies. After studying the adoption issue and experiencing the personal grief of a birth parent, I came to the decision that I could not adopt an infant whose mother might someday regret her decision as I did.*

*After some futile efforts to save our marriage, it ended. My difficulty accepting my infertility was intensified by my having given up a child to adoption. My relationship with the man I loved deteriorated partly because of this.*

*In hindsight, I would have gone to a counselor who specialized in helping infertile couples, as my gynecologist had suggested. I would have tried more openly to assure my husband that I needed and appreciated him for much more than his procreative potential. And last but not least, I would not have given my child away to strangers or to anyone else.*

*Would haves, unfortunately, won't help me change what has been done. My experience and the telling of it can hopefully help others better understand the interrelationship of being a birth parent and later being infertile.*

# Letter to The Kansas City Star

The following is a letter I sent to The Kansas City Star. I didn't have a date on it in my file, nor do I know if the Star published it.

*I am responding to the letter opposed to open adoption records in Missouri. It is a myth that opening records would increase abortions because birth parents would not have their promised confidentiality.*

*A recent Tennessee court case, "Doe v. Sundquist," outlined by attorney Erick Greenman in the American Adoption Congress Decree, says, "...we showed instead that approximately 95 percent of birth parents want to be contacted by their surrendered children."*

*The case disputes the notion that prior laws authorized promises to birth parents that their identities would be kept secret and that such promises were commonly made. In the lawsuit, it became clear that no such promise has ever been put in writing anywhere at any time.*

*Greenman sites clear evidence that open adoption records did not increase abortions in Kansas and Alaska, where adult adoptees have had unrestricted access to their original birth certificates for a long time.*

*Thousands of reunions have occurred without ruined lives, as predicted by secrecy advocates. I predict these reunions will continue to heal the parties involved and that open records in Missouri will decrease abortions.*

*I challenge caring and thinking citizens to contact their state legislators to support House Bill 1216.*

I see no signature to the above letter. I had many close relatives in Kansas City, and I probably wanted to stay in the closet as a birth mother. The bill mentioned in my letter was probably about letting adult adoptees access their original birth certificates rather than adoption records, something that many people, including myself, sometimes are confused about.

### The Missouri Adoptee Rights Act

Missouri legislators finally passed a law allowing adult adoptees to obtain a copy of their original birth certificates if there was no signed restriction form on file from a birth parent.

According to the Missouri Department of Health and Senior Services website, "Under the Missouri Adoptee Rights Act (Section 193.125 and 193.128, RSMo), adoptees, adoptee's attorneys, birth parents, and lineal descendants of deceased adoptees can request a copy of the adoptee's original birth certificate. The copy will be non-certified and will be stamped with "For genealogical purposes only. Not to be used for establishing identity"." As of this writing, the act provides that both adoptees and birth parents have the option to complete a contact preference form stating if they would like to be contacted or not.

# Paper for my College English Class

English 20 Section 61 Final Draft Paper #2 10/6/94

(Instructor's marks in parentheses and italics; my original text in [brackets])

A Birth Mother SPEAKS:

UNSEAL MY DAUGHTER'S BIRTH CERTIFICATE (*good title!*)

One of the most famous adoptees, Moses, must have had a strong need to make a connection with the family of his birth. After he was raised by an Egyptian Pharaoh's daughter, he led his people, the Jews, out of slavery back to their homeland. If the knowledge of his birth had been kept from Moses then, as it is for the majority of adoptees in the United States today, the Jewish people would have had a much different history. *(good intro!)*

My interest in adoption began a few months before I became a birth parent and signed relinquishment papers terminating my parental rights to my four day old daughter. *(hyphens)*. I now realize that the secrecy surrounding adoption records and in particular, the practice of sealing original birth certificates, can have very negative consequences for those directly involved: the birth parents, the adoptee, and the adoptive parents.

At the time of my daughter's birth and adoption I was not given copies of any documents.

When I signed the release of parental rights in the judge's private chambers with the adoptive parents' lawyer eagerly waiting nearby, I couldn't read the paper I was signing because of my tears and grief at the time. It didn't occur to me to ask for a copy, and *(I)* probably wouldn't have been given one anyway. Why is it that I get copies of everything else I sign in this life, from student loans to gas purchases? Parents are usually given birth certificates of their children. I was my daughter's legal parent at the time of her birth, but I'm denied a copy of it. *(watch out for vague "its" "her certificate")* Somehow this *(it)* would make it *(her birth)* seem more real that it was *(to have it)* acknowledged by society in some way. As a psychiatric nurse, I now know that denying the reality of something painful is not healthy. For years it *(the pregnancy? the loss of your daughter?)* was like a bad dream, something hazy and sad, but frequently in the back of my mind. At the time of my daughter's birth I wasn't allowed to see her or even to know her sex.

About fifteen years ago I asked my gynecologist to request my hospital records, which he did and then kindly turned over to me. I remember sitting in fascination looking at the hospital record that detailed my baby's birth. A picture of her formed in my mind as I read that she weighed five pounds and fifteen ounces, breathed spontaneously, and was "grossly normal." The verification of the reality of her birth may seem like an insignificant thing to some *(one who has never had a child, to me as a mother, it)* was one of the beginning steps in my healing process as a mother who has lost her child. *(relate this to then} "why did I have to wait 15 years to learn that my baby was a girl? The records were available; my healing could have begun years ago…")*

Today in most states, except Kansas and Alaska, the original birth certificate of an adopted infant is "sealed," which means it's filed somewhere in a state building and cannot be seen by anyone but the file-keepers and other bureaucrats. My daughter, her adoptive parents, and I are denied access. At the time of adoption, an amended *(birth)* certificate is created with the adoptive parents' names in place of the names of the birth parents.

In many instances, the location of birth and other information can be changed or deleted. *(this is psychologically damaging:)* Many adoptees say they feel like they were never born because they don't know the true facts of their birth. They express feelings of not being fully connected to the human race because they have biological and personality characteristics that seem out of place in their adoptive families, despite otherwise gratifying family ties.

Adoption agency personnel and parents often will not give adoptees identifying information, that is, actual names and other identifying information, such as addresses. In my daughter's case, she would not be able to see the birth certificate that has my or her birth father's *(This gets kind of dense — maybe focus on your name.)* name on it.

If my daughter wants to know about her origin and can't get identifying information from her parents, she *[would]* *(will)* have to get a court order or initiate what could be a time-consuming and expensive search to learn what non adopted persons take for granted, *(as stated in The Adoption Triangle by Sorosky, Baran, and Pannor 22-23) The [*reason*] (*practice*)* for sealing birth records was originally instituted to protect the adoptive family from intrusion by uninvolved persons *[*as stated in <u>The Adoption Triangle</u> by Sorosky, Baran, and Pannor 22-23.]* The authors explain that it's been a common assumption, however, to believe the reason for sealing records was to protect the adoptive family from disruption by the birth parents.

A further assumption [was] *(is)* that it *(a sealed record)* was a way to protect the birth mother from the shame of bearing a child out of wedlock *[*or from the unwanted disruption of her life by the child later on.] *(the birth mother would also be protected against unwanted disruption ...)* The adoptee would not have the stigma of ILLEGITIMATE stamped on their birth certificate or "unknown" typed in place of a father's name, as was the common practice. *(transition: However, these assumptions are false.)*

Birth family access to the original birth certificate would not cause disruption to the adoptive family since their names aren't on it. On the contrary, adoptees who have searched and found their birth families report a stronger bond with their adoptive families, not a disruption.

They often say how their curiosity about their origins is misinterpreted by their adoptive families as disloyalty and a desire to replace them. Such an attitude is reinforced by policies which seem to protect the adoptive families but, in reality, cause a rift of silence between parents and child. *(On the other hand, the search for birth parents can save adoptees and adoptive parents:)* I've seen many adoptive parents with their children at search and support group meetings and conferences who together are searching for birth families. It's clearly evident that their openness helps promote a close relationship.

I too want protection from uninvolved persons seeking personal information about me. My daughter, who is now twenty-five, should be protected from (outsiders) *[people outside her family and mine from]* knowing the circumstances of her birth. Certainly, she is a legitimate human being and doesn't deserve the insult of ILLEGITIMATE on any of her private documents. This *[practice]* *(label)* should be dropped if there are any states still *[doing]* *(using)* it. But this does not mean that *(personal)* information about herself should be kept from her. My purpose in placing her for adoption was to provide her with a family and opportunities I felt incapable of providing at the time, not to deprive her of anything, including knowledge of her ancestry.

Furthermore, if she wishes to use this information to search for me and find out about her birth family, I would be overjoyed to have this happen. I don't want outmoded practices to stand in her way. Protection could be maintained for birth parents who don't want to be found, and there are *[some]* *(some what? Forms of protection?)* by simply having an affidavit on file by those birth parents who do not want the record sealed. I have faith in the intelligence and resourcefulness of our public servants in state records departments to figure out a way to turn over records to people who are directly related to the documents, but not to others.

Registries are available for persons who seek others separated by adoption, but they are not widely publicized, and I worry my daughter might not know about them. Since my daughter's adoption was arranged privately through an attorney who is now dead, she has no agency to go to for information like many adoptees do. Her parents might feel too threatened they'll lose her to even discuss it.

*(Making)* *[Unsealing]* the original birth certificate *(available)* to the main parties in adoption should be enacted in every state. It's an important key element in beginning a search for the birth family. If you believe original birth records should be opened to those directly involved, join me and others in the adoption reform movement. Information about adoption activist groups in most areas can be obtained by contacting The American Adoption Congress in Washington, D.C.

As for me, I hope to one day meet my daughter and know more about her than I do now. I pray her adoptive parents will not see me as a threat, but as a person *[interested]* like them, *(interested)* in what is best for her. Our daughter may not have the distinction of leading the people of her ancestral roots to the Promised Land, like Moses did, but I hope someday she'll get the rich history of her German-American family starting with her first birth certificate.

# A Letter for Possible Publication

I am not sure if the following piece was ever read by legislators, but it was written specifically to them. Because adoption laws vary from state to state, there were efforts in many states to enact laws to give adoptees rights to their original birth certificates. I recall writing a letter at the request of New Jersey adoption reform activists to boost their argument that birth mothers did not want privacy from their own children they had placed for adoption. This particular document is directed toward Missouri legislators.

*February 15, 2009*

### *My Experience as a Birth Mother as it Relates to Access to Records by Judy Bock*

*When I became pregnant in 1968 at the age of 21, I felt panic. I was not married and did not want to marry the father. I never considered abortion, although I later learned other women I knew personally chose this option.*

*I knew no one in my family or circle of friends and acquaintances who was a single mother. At the time I had just started my first job as a registered nurse and was living in a studio apartment with a girlfriend. I could not see myself parenting a child at that time although I'd hoped to have many children some day. I found it incredibly difficult to tell my parents about my situation. I grew up in a small Missouri town and was raised in a very religious, Catholic family of eight children. I knew it would be a great embarrassment to my family, and I feared the disgrace I would feel in their eyes.*

*A friend suggested I consider adoption and to come live with her in another state. This I chose to do, and except for one sister, I kept the pregnancy a secret from my family until many years later. I had a baby who weighed 5 pounds and 15 ounces. I was not allowed to see her or hold her. I did not know I had the right to do that, and now wish I had been able to. I also wish that I'd been able to meet the people who would parent my child.*

*A private, non-agency adoption was arranged through an attorney who represented a couple who had come to my doctor's office. I do not recall being told much about them other than that they could provide a good life for my child. I trusted my doctor and signed away my parental rights when she was four days old. Confidentiality was never discussed. It was just assumed and treated as a private matter. There was a "No-Show, No-Tell" warning on my hospital chart. Had I been asked if my child could someday know my name, I would have said yes.*

*I grieved for that child but avoided dealing with it until much later. I eventually went to counseling and became educated in post-adoption issues through organizations such as the American Adoption Congress and Concerned United Birthparents. I learned many adoptees want to know about their roots, and many want to meet their birth families.*

*I searched for my daughter and found her when she was about 16. After going through all the avenues through the state (Oklahoma) as well as search groups without success, I paid a private investigator $xxxx and got her name, her parents' names and her address. Without* contacting her then, I satisfied my need to know that she was well, happy and in a good home. When she was 18, I sent her a letter. I have had sporadic phone contact with her over the years, but she doesn't want a reunion. Perhaps someday she will change her mind. I do have the comforting knowledge that she was raised by a good family, had a good education and seems happy. I have a photo of her and her four children.

Adoptees and birth parents who want to know something of each other and perhaps meet each other in person are often thwarted by complicated laws in the state of Missouri. Birth parents seem to have no method of searching through the state registry, were they to even know of its existence. Laws give the state registry personnel no process for helping us birth parents. Adoptees are encumbered by a ridiculous caveat to get their adoptive parents' permission to seek a reunion under Missouri law. They should not need to do this as adults.

I understand that some birth parents may fear exposure and embarrassment if adopted adults were given access to their original birth certificates and adoption papers in the archives of the state. It is my experience in my 40-plus years in adoption search and support groups that adoptees and birth parents who have sought reunions are very discreet in making contact.

Knowledge of their relationship need not go beyond the adoptee and the birth parent.

In many cases, the birth parent would be overjoyed to have such contact. For those who do not want it, the right of refusal is available to them, like any person who does not want a relationship with another person. The fear of catastrophic results should adoptees have access to records is not the reality in other states where records are *available to adult adoptees upon request: Kansas, Alaska, Oregon, New Hampshire, Maine and Alabama.*

*Updated and current health information that birth families can share with adoptees is also very important to consider. I believe the current laws related to access to records for adoptees and birth parents in the state of Missouri are unjust, and thwart the very human and normal need for wholeness and family ties every person needs. Surely Missouri can show us who chose adoption and those who were adopted more mercy.*

# Writing Journal Notes (My Complaint Log)

The following "present day" notes are miscellaneous entries to my writing journal, also my complaint log. They helped me get out some of my frustrations with the project and greased the mental juices that needed priming in order to crank out more words each day of writing.

Another feature of my log is that it gives a look into my day-to-day life for the last few years within my family. I have finally found what I had always thought I wanted, namely a role as wife to a loving husband with whom I could share many interests and being a mother of sorts as a stepmom and a pet parent.

**Present Day**

*Early spring 2019*

*I am feeling rushed to get my 300 words in. Oh wait, was it supposed to be 500? My present life of retirement is overscheduled, to be sure. I need to simplify it. If I am going to get this book finished before I die, I will need to make it a priority rather than just one more thing to cross off my list of tasks. (Note during subsequent editing: This never happened.) But spring is here, and flowers and vegetables need to be planted. Climate change is threatening the earth, and my volunteer work with Citizens Climate Lobby seems urgent. Recently I was at a Zoom meeting with the leader of our local group and city administrators in Washington, Missouri, to get something started in their town. Back to my memoir.*

**Present Day**

*April 5, 2019*

*Today I delayed some household chores, emptying the dishwasher, walking the dog, and looking at vacation plans so that I would get in* my two pages of writing. Two pages, 35 minutes; my writing guidelines are flexible. I'll be taking a trip in the fall with two high school buddies, something we try to do every year or so. It's a cloudy but relatively warm April day here in Missouri. The winter of 2018-2019 was somewhat brutal, with lots of snow, ice and cold. It's great to see the daffodils and hyacinths blooming all over. Even the magnolia trees have started their short-lived blossoming. Its two days from Rose Diane's birthday and three days from mine.

### Present Day

*April 13, 2019*

It's a gorgeous spring day in spring 2019, and I'd really rather be out walking Lily than sitting down at this computer. I survived Rose's birthday five days ago just fine, without sadness or even wondering if she thought of me on her birthday. Well, that's not entirely true. I did have a fleeting thought about how she must be relieved that I didn't send her a birthday card. She had received one from me every birthday for years. It was always a challenge to pick one for her. So far, Hallmark and other card makers don't have a section in card racks for birth and adoptive family relationships. The cards I sent were usually rather generic.

But I will press on with my goal of writing a couple of pages, or 300 words, as Anne LaMotte suggests writers do every day. Rosie, our eight-year-old cat, has settled on my lap and looks at me with her blue eyes. I used to discourage her insistence on getting on my lap while I tried to write, but have given in to her unrelenting need to be near. Our pets have truly filled a vacuum. My husband and I call them our children and even joke about characteristics they have "inherited" from us.

*April 24, 2019*

*My life and volunteer efforts, such as action against climate change, exercises for my spinal stenosis (which changed to simple hip joint arthritis), walking the dog while listening to a book, park patrol volunteer on the city nature trail and the usual duties of cooking, cleaning and laundry, are getting in the way of my resolve to keep writing this memoir. I just needed to get that off my chest to lubricate my journalism juices. Bird by bird...*

***Present Day***

*May 2, 2019*

*I didn't write yesterday. I spent some time potting flowers and other horticultural pursuits in the afternoon. I prepped for a Zoom conference coming up for a Citizens Climate Lobby meeting with city leaders from Washington, Missouri. Then I took my sister to lunch at our favorite Chinese buffet. She is 84 now and living in a small, friendly assisted living facility. Today I got an early start and feel fresher than usual, both in mind and body.*

***Present Day***

*May 30, 2019*

*Breaking for real time life events, I want to let you know about my recent experience with Mother's Day earlier this month. Probably anticipating my sadness because of Rose emphatically declining a second meeting, my dear husband made sure Mother's Day would be special anyway. He focused on our pet children and bought cards from both Lily and Rosie. Both were humorously adorned with pink bows and were presented along with gifts of a hanging flower basket and two bottles of wine. I voiced doubt that they could have independently shopped for these things, so Glenn told me they had instructed him what to buy.*

*We spent a good portion of the day shopping for a new front door and storm/screen door, something I had expressed I wanted when he asked what I wanted for Mother's Day. Later he fixed a barbeque chicken dinner with typical American sides of baked beans, lettuce salad, corn on the cob and watermelon for dessert. Stepson Jim and granddaughter Tina joined us for dinner to make it a complete family day.*

*I didn't think much about Rose as sometimes in the past. It feels like a closed subject for the most part. She made it clear that she has a great family because of her adoption and really has no interest in pursuing a relationship with me.*

### Present Day

*Sometime in June 2019*

*I have had an epiphany of sorts as far as my writing regimen. Often, I am plagued with insomnia, especially after relieving my post-menopausal bladder and subsequent sleeplessness in the middle of the night. Lately, I have gone to the bathroom around 4 a.m. and then lay there, unsuccessful at returning to sleep. This morning I realized I might as well get up and sit at my laptop until I have accomplished my 300 to 500 words. So here I am.*

*I am leaving on a trip later this morning to gather with my three sisters at an Airbnb in central Missouri. Luckily, we are heading away from any rivers or flooded roads during this year of massive flooding along the Missouri and Arkansas rivers.*

**Present Day**

*About a week later*

*Recently I have had numerous interruptions in my current life that have truly prevented me from getting to my laptop. One was the two-overnight at a rental house via Airbnb for a reunion with my three sisters. We never turned on the TV. We cooked all our meals, played Scrabble and cards, watched the sunset from the front porch and reminisced while going through family photos. On the way back home, three of us visited with our oldest brother, now in his late 80's, who is caring for his ailing wife.*

*Then I had volunteer work one day at a thrift shop, and was busy with normal household responsibilities. I couldn't seem to carve out any uninterrupted time. Now, where was I in this book?*

**Present Day**

*July 11, 2019.*

*I have been busy as usual and have not found time, or made time to write in several days.*

*Once last week, I had trouble sleeping and finally opened my laptop to work on this writing project. Fortunately, my life is filled with family and volunteer activities that keep me from getting bored or depressed about losses and disappointments in my life.*

*One recent fun event was going to a local theater for a big screen live viewing of the Women's World Cup final two games in which the U.S. won the trophy. Another big event was the long anticipated retirement of my husband. I enjoyed attending a luncheon for him with his boss and coworkers. More importantly, we had a visit at our home with my stepdaughter, her husband and two young boys. I find myself more willing to be fully present and engaged in their visits. I like blowing bubbles and playing ping pong and wiffle ball with the eight-year-old and two-year-old, both of whom seem to like grandma a lot more than a year ago.*

*I sometimes wonder if my realization that I need to give fully to the family I have isn't a big part of an inward change for the better. Ironically, Rose probably did me a favor in declining my offer to form a continuing relationship. I would have had room for her in my life, but this new freedom, I feel, is a welcome trade.*

### *Present-day*

*August 6, 2019*

*I confess that I haven't been doing my writing as intended, bird by bird, day by day.*

*Mostly good things are interfering with my best intentions.*

*My life is very fulfilling these days, despite the disappointment in my effort to form a relationship with Rose.*

*My husband recently retired, and the kids and I hosted a retirement party at our home.*

*We had about 30 people, mostly family, a neighbor and friends. Many people regretfully declined due to previously made plans. It was a fun day with a whole ping pong table full of sandwiches, macaroni and potato salads, five pies, deviled eggs, veggies and dip, chips and non-alcoholic drinks.*

*People ambled upstairs, downstairs and out onto the covered patio and yard. Four yard games were set up, and the competition was heaviest on corn bag toss (called corn hole here in mid-Missouri), washers (another tossing game) and last but not least, red-neck golf, the latter of which is yet another tossing game of golf balls on each end of a short rope tossed toward three levels of horizontal bars on a stand.*

*I enjoyed talking with everyone as I went to the various locations and seeing that Glenn was having a good time amid his kids, grandkids, friends and even a great-grandchild. It was mostly organized and prepared by Glenn's youngest child with help from the rest of the kids and me. I didn't feel the absence of my daughter. In fact, if anything, I felt closer to my stepdaughter than ever as we worked together to get things ready. We had even had a shopping trip for much of the food and then went out to lunch a couple days prior to the event.*

*Other highlights in my life include fun times with the grandkids. We took two of them to a big aquatic center in a nearby town for an afternoon. We hosted our step granddaughter for a couple of days and had lots of fun, intentionally spoiling her with a movie, dinner out and other fun activities. I enjoyed having a 16-year-old grandson at our home for several days recently. He got more driving experience with Papa, and we celebrated his getting his driver's license, ate well, went to a movie and played cards among other work and play activities.*

*Speaking of birds, an Eastern bluebird couple have nested in our bluebird box in our backyard. I watched them build the nest over a period of several days. I believe the eggs are incubating now with the mother bird sitting on the eggs.*

*I love watching monarch butterflies in our neighbors' and our yards, where we have purposely planted milkweed for their benefit. We've seen a few scattered monarch caterpillars as well as some beautiful swallowtails adding to the many miracles of nature surrounding us.*

*Suppose this bucolic description of my current life sounds too much like a combination of a Pollyanna type Hallmark theme. In that case, it may be my effort to give proof to you, my reader, and even myself that my life is full of things and people that make me happy despite my loss of Rose.*

*My volunteer activities also keep me busy. I am part of an all-volunteer staff at a local thrift store near our downtown. Our main service is to low income families and individuals referred to the store for free clothing and bedding and to school children in financial need to get new school shoes twice a year. The store sells gently used and sometimes new clothing and shoes and a few household items at rock bottom prices to the general public as well. I often avail myself of this perk as my fellow volunteers do.*

*I serve on the board as the publicity coordinator, something for which my journalism degree prepared me. I also help sort donations and put them out on the selling floor.*

*More about my current life later. The point I want to get across again is that I don't feel an immense void in my life most of the time. I have family, friends and enough activities to keep me more than busy and fulfilled. I would, however, make room for Rose if she were to want me in her life, however much or little.*

### Present Day

*August 23, 2019*

*I am writing on the picnic table on the downstairs patio and under the ceiling fan.*

*I really don't think of Rose too much, although from time to time, the reality of her and my birth motherhood comes to mind. I continue to feel that she's done me a favor in a sense by releasing me from the hope that we could forge a continuing relationship. My life seems to have settled into a happy (usually) rhythm of sorts. My husband has retired, and we are doing fine so far with our closer proximity throughout the day.*

*This morning, for instance, I got up about an hour and a half before he did, puttered around the house, refreshing floral bouquets, iced the orchids, started the coffee and a skillet rice/veggie/egg breakfast for myself and fed the cat. I eventually shared the rice concoction with him, did my back exercises, and puttered about some more.*

*He's out on the city trail on his new bike, and I'm happily writing in a lovely environment that we have filled with plants, a hammock, a glider, picnic table and a lounge chair. I've texted my sister and niece and sent a photo of my idyllic writing scene, and they've responded with friendly thoughts. I can hear the cicadas rising and falling chorus. Other than climate change threatening the human species and literally the entire living world as we know it, life is good.*

*On a bit of a lighter but sad note, our bluebird nesting family that we've been watching the last few weeks has had a tragic end. At the beginning of August, a couple of eastern bluebirds mated at the end of fledgling season and built a nest in the box on our backyard fence. The mother laid four beautiful blue eggs, and both proud parents chased squirrels and other birds away from the birdhouse whenever they felt their brood was threatened. While the mother returned faithfully to sit on the eggs during the incubation time, we stopped seeing the daddy, and he never returned. We knew the babies had hatched when we saw mother bluebird bringing worms and bugs to the box.*

*I peeked into the nest box one day when I was sure the mother was out looking for food and saw the sweet little birds, at least three, cozy in the nest. We became worried yesterday when we realized the mother had not been seen for over 24 hours. Our anxiety grew when we saw little open beaks repeatedly poking out from the dark hole of the birdhouse.*

*I checked the local Audubon Facebook page and eventually got referred to a songbird rehabilitation volunteer. She came last evening to attempt a rescue of the three starving little birds. A fourth had died, possibly from hypothermia or starvation. She had a syringe of baby food fruit that two of the little birds accepted. A third was not as strong and wouldn't open its beak for the fruit puree. The volunteer promised to text updates, but I haven't heard from her. I texted her just now.*

*So, you get an idea of my everyday life. It goes on just fine despite occasional wildlife tragedies and normal ups and downs of life.*

**Present Day**

*September 2, 2019*

*I returned from a trip to the state of Oregon two days ago, having traveled with two friends from boarding school days, Mary and Susie. They had been boarders like me and were also from Missouri. We've maintained a post high school friendship through the years that gets renewed with trips in the United States the last few years.*

*During the Oregon trip with my girlfriends, we walked on the beach for miles, gathered smooth stones and mussel shells, talked and laughed a lot. We sampled the local eateries, bars and shops. We did our part to help with the American economy at stores ranging from Goodwill to Coach, buying matching black and white striped tops at Chico's. When we wore them one day on a tour to Mount Hood, we got lots of favorable comments and smiles about our matching attire. We told a few of the folks who approached us that we were identical triplets, which brought chuckles.*

*We visited the Portland Japanese garden and the rose research garden just across the street. Roses were still in bloom. They were beautiful and smelled fantastic. In the past, I had honored my daughter Rose by collecting all sorts of things, from jewelry to clothing, with images of roses or rose in the name. I suspect I thought of Rose there in the garden.*

*The prevalence of homeless people of all ages of adulthood in a lot of the parks and commercial areas of Portland saddened us. Once when having a bite in a Chinese café, we were told we had just missed seeing a naked man running down the busy street outside. We learned a woman had done the same a day before. We were only mildly surprised by this and perversely thankful that we witnessed no mass shootings as is currently happening at too frequent intervals in this great country that is not really great again and never has been entirely for some disadvantaged groups.*

*As Mary and Susie spoke of their children and grandchildren, I spoke of my children and grandchildren by marriage. I briefly had passing thoughts of my biological child, but she and her children do not figure into my social conversations.*

*Life has resumed in a much more predictable manner since my return home. We had a niece and her new husband for a meal and visit the night of my return home from Oregon, the meal being prepared entirely by my husband. I was allowed to unpack and put my feet up until the guests arrived but cleaned up the kitchen after they left.*

*We attended my hometown pre-Labor Day parish picnic and saw numerous friends and relatives there. I had one quiet moment at the Bingo stand when I thought about what it would have been like had I kept Rose Diane, and she and her children would have no doubt been at the event with me. But that, too, was fleeting and saddened me only slightly. I am blessed not to be in continual grief about losing her. But let it be repeated; I would be more than willing to resume the adventure of getting to know each other if Rose ever changes her mind.*

### Present Day

*Fall of 2019*

*I had to combat a lot of resistance to sit down at my desk to write today. Partly I am just tired, although seven hours of fairly solid sleep should have been enough. I am realizing every day that getting old is a constellation of physical challenges, lack of energy sometimes being*

230

one of them. This morning on the radio, there was a report of the state of Missouri being close to the first state to have no abortion facilities providing the procedure. My thinking on abortion is conflicted. When I had my crisis pregnancy, I never considered having an abortion. Had someone suggested I do, I honestly don't think that I would have, even though I felt pretty desperate about my situation. But on to my story...

**Present Day**

*September 10, 2019*

*I really, really don't want to write today. It seems this is a common complaint of mine. I have not been wanting to write for many days. Did I get off track with my nearly week-long trip to Oregon? Was it the nights I haven't been sleeping well lately? Laziness, low energy, emotional drag of bringing submerged and difficult memories to the forefront of my mind? Probably all of these and other reasons I haven't thought of yet.*

*Over the weekend, I participated in an event to raise awareness and seek action to combat climate change. I talked to numerous people and asked them to sign up to call their legislators to make policy changes to decrease fossil fuel use. The ultimate goal at this point is zero fossil fuel emissions by 2050 after a gradual transition to environmentally sustainable production.*

*Should I live that long I would be 101 years old. I'm not really sure I want to inhabit my failing, often aching body that long.*

*I tell people that I am trying to do something about climate change to ease the guilt I feel about leaving the earth in such a sorry condition for my grandchildren. My mind makes a momentary flight to the question of which of my grandchildren I am talking about, the four biological grandkids or the ones granted to me through my marriage. The answer, of course, is both. If they ever read this, I hope they will know I did it for them especially, and humanity in general. It's an ethical, moral issue for me, the ultimate pro-life crusade.*

*So some of my activities take my time and energy away from writing. I just need to get back into the habit of sitting down for a half hour or more most days. Once I start typing, I generally lose track of time and enjoy the flow of sending my thoughts out into the world despite how flawed my strivings might be.*

*Following the entries in my notebook and writing about my search and reunion has not been too difficult, although I have complained repeatedly. It's moving slowly, bird by bird. Many of us less than perfect humans simply try to put one foot in front of the other, day after day, and have some sort of purpose to our existence.*

### *Present Day*

*November 6, 2019*

*I have not made it to my keyboard for quite some time now. The reason, other than my over-committing myself, is a somewhat lazy mindset about writing. I am not one of those writers who has a strong need to record my thoughts in some way every day, although I have been known to journal on an irregular basis.*

*Another factor is that Glenn and I bought Lily a new doghouse in September. Let me elaborate. As designated in the camper retail business, it's an RV, a Class C motorhome. In the classification system, it's two steps behind the huge Class A motorhomes that you might have seen on interstate highways and wonder what big music*

232

*star and her band is touring in it. Then there's the Class B van-type camper which is much smaller than ours. It's a van with an elevated roof and equipped with many accessories needed for camping, but often missing the important toilet for those middle-of-the-night visits Glenn and I both need to make.*

*Prior to getting the RV, we missed having our pets, our fur-children, when we went on vacations. We felt bad leaving Rosie, our cat, to fend for herself except for brief visits from a friend or a neighbor, and Lily had to go to "puppy prison" for too long of a boarding period.*

*Our motorhome, named Ramona, the Roamer, has an illustration of a spotted dog decorating several areas on its exterior. So the occasional reference to a new dog house for Lily is often the preamble to telling friends and family about our RV purchase. Lily is not spotted, but most definitely a dog capable of leaping.*

*Our recent first big trip in Ramona was in the late fall of this year to the warmer weather of Arkansas, not far from my sister Barbara who we visited. Notably, we passed right through Rose Diane's town on the way and were, in fact, only a few miles away from her home.*

*Not appreciating being brought along, Rosie kept us up much of the first night with uncharacteristic loud meowing and trying to get out the door to go home. Lily slept fine in her kennel between the driver and passenger seat up front until Rosie woke her up along with the rest of us. Somehow we made it through that first night with enough sleep to start the new camping day with enthusiasm, a fresh pot of coffee and a nice breakfast cooked in the tiny but adequate RV kitchen.*

*The next night went better, with almost no meowing, and we all slept pretty well. The pets seemed to get along better than at home, possibly because there wasn't as much chasing room for Lily to pursue the cat on a dead run and tackle her like a football player. Glenn and I enjoyed reading books, napping, playing cards, and a visit to a winery. We discovered a panoramic view of the Ozark mountains on a hilltop overlooking St. Mary's church near Altus.*

*One of the highlights was a day-long visit with my sister, who allowed me to beat her at Scrabble in the last play of the game.*

*I must say that my mothering needs are somewhat fulfilled with having these two pets.*

*Not that it makes up for not having human children. But in a way, it is a good substitute. Glenn is daddy to the pets, and I am mommy, as we often refer to each other, especially when talking to the pets or in activities involving them. "Say good night to mommy," Glenn will say prior to putting Lily in her kennel for "nite nite." (Yes, baby talk often surfaces when interacting with pets.) She will come to me willingly, sometimes needing some prompting, for a brief petting and ear rubbing from me and then go to her kennel. Most pet lovers know the pleasure of having their mere arrival after an absence being greeted with excited enthusiasm by a beloved dog.*

*Even Rosie will often come to greet us when we enter the house or, in this case, the RV.*

### Present Day

*February 7, 2020*

*It has been several weeks since I've sat at my computer. In the meantime, I have had several medical tests that eventually placed me* in an operating room on January 28th for a triple coronary artery bypass operation, a significant milestone in my life.

I had only been having vague pressure-like pains in my left chest that I felt at night when lying still. Perhaps I was more tired than usual, but I had thought old age was just exhibiting its normal progression. My husband told me that I'd been notably slowing down during our walks on the hiking-biking trail or around the neighborhood.

Deciding to have the operation was based on evidence and options available from my cardiologist and a cardiac surgeon. I had over 78% blockage in my right coronary artery and inconveniently located blockages of a lesser percentage in my left descending artery and the circumflex branching off from it. Stents were an unfavorable option in my case because of the location of the blockages and characteristics of the latter two. Medical management was offered but not strongly recommended, as the bypass by far the desirable option recommended by my cardiologist.

One must decide whether to trust the experts or not. Their credentials were good. The reputation of the heart center where both doctors practiced, and the hospital's heart program had top ratings for the state.

So I was admitted at 5:30 a.m. on a Tuesday for the operation, had one night in ICU and spent three days and nights on the specialty cardiology floor. I progressed well enough to be discharged home under Glenn's care on my fourth postop day.

I got lots of attention for this medical adventure from family and friends, who showered me with gifts, cards and promises of prayers. Glenn sent updates by email and sometimes texts. He told me later that had I not made it through surgery or at some point soon after, he *would have notified Rose, despite her recent firm command to stop any communication.*

*I had thought of her briefly during the pre and post operative period. It would be beneficial to know this medical history so that she could make changes in her diet or other lifestyle choices to avoid a similar path. But I still felt the sting of her emphatic desire to hear nothing further from me. Glenn, of course, would not have been bound by this.*

*With the showering of love and renewed connections within our immediate family, along with those of my extended family, numerous true friends who let me know how concerned they were, I didn't feel the absence of my daughter in my life at such an important time.*

*I now have a daughter through my marriage to Glenn, who sent me one of the prettiest floral bouquets I have seen in a long time and who texted me frequently to find out how I was feeling each day.*

*My sons and grandchildren, through marriage, were worried about me in a way I didn't realize they would be. As soon as I was ready, they and their families came to visit me at home to see in person that I was going to be OK. Our oldest son took a rare day off and supported his dad with his presence through the entire operative day at the hospital.*

*I did not mourn the loss of Rose at that time nor today as I write this. I have moved on, finally. At least, I am telling myself that. Would I welcome her into my heart and life in the unlikely event that she changed her mind at some point in the future? Sure I would.*

**Present Day**

*April 13, 2020*

*Rose's and my birthdays have come and gone, hers on April 7th and mine on the 8th, as it does every year. Easter was a couple of days ago.*

*Diane, who had been in the delivery room with me, texted on Rose's birthday, "Hi honey, thinking of you today. Wishing I could give you a big hug & kiss."*

*I had thought of Rose as her birthday came, but honestly realized it wasn't uppermost in my mind when I got the text from Diane. I do hope and pray she and her family are safe from the pandemic. But my immediate thoughts concern my present life in my home and that of my stepchildren, who seem to be more and more a part of my life. One son even texted me this year, "Happy birthday mama, hope you have a great day. Hope dad's fixing you a good meal."*

*And indeed he did, two in fact. Eggs Benedict for breakfast, homemade cinnamon rolls for whenever, and a smoked chicken dinner from the home grill.*

*I did not send Rose a birthday card as I had in many years of her adulthood once I knew her address. I have been thinking though, that I should inform her in a quick note about my triple bypass. She should know that her biological mother has coronary artery disease. It would be the right thing to do to inform her. I would be asking nothing of her, just giving her health information.*

*How coincidental that one of my brothers, Gerry, died of a massive heart attack at the age of 72 on April 11, 2011. He'd been having chest pain but thought it was indigestion. He left early from the first tennis game of the year with some buddies, probably because*

237

*of the increasing pain and his need to make a deposit at the bank. He died in the drive-thru after making the deposit. He was the same age I was when I had my triple bypass, and his symptom of chest pain was there while he played a game both Rose and I liked to play.*

### *Present Day*

*April 16, 2021*

*I haven't been on my Chromebook to continue editing or proofreading the manuscript of this book since April 5, 2021. We were on our RV trip to escape the late winter cold in Missouri for the warmer weather of the Mississippi Gulf Coast.*

*Both vaccinated and trusting we were immune to Covid-19, Glenn and I enjoyed eating inside a few restaurants and went to the Mississippi Aquarium and the Ohr-O'Keefe Museum of Art in cities close to our campground in Ocean Springs. We continued to mask and mostly social distanced per CDC guidance, as were most of the Mississippi locals.*

*We walked on the sands of the Gulf Coast beaches, all open to the public, and hiked and biked when the intermittent rains permitted. We marveled at sightings of three alligators of various sizes, estimated lengths of three to twelve feet, in several bayous near our campground but far enough away to give us a sense of safety.*

*Generally, I found the people we encountered warm and friendly, not too different from the people in Missouri. I am aware that we have the relative privilege of being white in mostly white owned businesses and tourist venues. Had we been people of color, we probably wouldn't be camping and might not have felt as welcome everywhere we went. But we did see people of color camping, and I hope they were treated equal to us.*

*Unfortunately, I got little done on my book project while on this trip. So now I resume after getting caught up with many areas of life neglected during our time away.*

*I have resumed weekly Scrabble with friend Cindy in our homes. We are both vaccinated.*

*I sympathized with her this week after the death of her beloved dog Maggie.*

*In my own family, my 84-year-old brother Maurice is very ill and in and out of the hospital after a fall in his home. He is rehabilitating in a long-term facility near his home and children in the Kansas City area.*

*Glenn's sister Alma's health is deteriorating mentally and physically. We went to visit her and her husband in her suburban St. Louis home yesterday and enjoyed a lunch buffet with them.*

*There is a new great nephew and more babies, hopefully in the production stage, as well as weddings, graduations and grandchildren circling our lives. So life continues onward, and we are planning our next RV trip in May. This time to Arkansas to visit sister Barbara and visit the northwestern corner of Arkansas with its world-class Crystal Bridges art museum and the Razorback Greenway hiking/biking trail. We will pass within a few miles of Rose's home without stopping, as we have numerous times before.*

***Present Day***

*May 27, 2021*

*Because of the close association between pregnancy, sex and intimate relationships, I struggle with what to gloss over or include. I am trying to be honest about it all so that others can more completely understand my emotional and psychological path as a birth mother.*

*I have a new life now, and I love my husband, children (by marriage) and grandchildren.*

*I hope they, and others who know me, won't be too shocked to read some of the things I've written.*

*If anything, this book is more to explain things to my daughter and her children, who may or may not ever read it. It's for the young parents who may be deciding what to do about an untimely pregnancy. It's for the counselors, social workers, pastors, priests and others to get an inside view of a birth mother's experience so that they will advise and guide with eyes wide open. And, of course, it was for me, probably most of all, to try to make more sense of why I gave my daughter away.*

# Searching on my Own

While attending various conferences and meetings of triad groups and organizations, I gathered lots of tips and abundant advice on searching. One of the recommendations was to register in the International Soundex Reunion Registry (ISRR) International Soundex Reunion Registry - ISRR . According to its web site, it is a non-profit, tax exempt, humanitarian service — reuniting families since 1975. People who are trying to find others in their biological family can register for free, and if the person they are looking for also registers, they can get the contact information of the other party and meet or correspond. It's kind of a slow ancestry.com, which has, in many cases, sped up adoption triad searches.

Some states also had reunion registries. But many people simply were, and are, unaware of the existence of registries or just aren't actively searching. Often if found and contacted, many who hadn't been searching were receptive to contact, often by phone or letter and eventually in person. Many TV news and magazines featured stories of happy reunions.

So I was hopeful that would also be the case for me and my daughter.

One of my first attempts at getting information from government offices was a letter to the Tulsa County Clerk June 30, 1981.

*Dear County Clerk,*

*I am requesting information as to any court proceedings or legal action taken regarding my daughter, Baby Girl Bock (I had not named her on the birth certificate. I simply was not asked what name to give my baby. I didn't know I had that right.) beginning on April 1969 and ending April 1971.*

*She, Baby Girl Bock, was at that time a minor having been born on April 7, 1969. Please bill me for any costs incurred in the copying of records sent to me.*

*Sincerely,*

*Judy Bock*

I got a brief typed response on the bottom of the above letter.

*I'm sorry I cannot determine what type of records you need. If it is an adoption, these matters are confidential and we can only release information with an Order from the Court. If you could please specify what type of records you wish, maybe we could be of service to you.*

It was signed by the Deputy Court Clerk.

It took a few months, but I sent a follow up letter on October 19 of that year.

*Dear Ms. xxxxxxx,*

*I am requesting from your office the name and address, if known, of the lawyer who handled the adoption of my daughter, Baby Girl Bock, who I surrendered through private adoption following her birth on April 7, 1969. I am also requesting copies of the surrender papers, which were not given to me at the time I signed them or at any subsequent time.*

*If you are unable to comply with these requests, I would like the name of the judge and court of jurisdiction that I can petition.*

*Sincerely,*

*Judy Bock*

I got a hand-written response, the bottom of which was cut off in the copy I kept, so it is incomplete. I believe it to be from Judge Jane P. Wiseman of District Court, as I wrote a subsequent letter to a lawyer who was referred by Judge Wiseman.

Nov. 7, 1981

*Dear Ms. Camera,*

*I'm sorry I'm so late in replying to your request. The attorney who handled this adoption was Mrs. Jean ..., here in Tulsa. I cannot release copies of the adoption papers since state law requires that these be held confidential. You might wish ...* (I believe the rest was instructions to contact that attorney. The letter I wrote to the lawyer follows.)

*December 3, 1981*

*Dear Mrs. Xxxx,*

*Your name and address have been forwarded to me by Judge Jane P. Wiseman of District Court. I am requesting your help regarding a child I surrendered through adoption after her birth on April 7, 1969. My name at that time was Bock and the doctor was Dr. James T. Maddox.*

*It is my request that you contact this child's adoptive parents to inform them that I would like to be available now or in the future to the child, and her parents to answer any questions or provide any information that they might seek in order to help her come to a full understanding of her background and heritage and the reasons for her release for adoption. This may be essential to building a strong and secure basis for her feelings about herself and her identity which is especially important as she enters her teen years.*

*I am further seeking, for my own peace of mind, to obtain non-identifying information regarding this child and her family — for example her health, school progress, brothers and sisters, problems etc. I know I am legally not entitled to this, but nonetheless I make the request on a purely human level.*

*In the event that you or the parents for whatever reason do not respond to my requests, I will continue to pursue my goals by other means.*

*You have my permission to release my name, address, and phone number to this child's parents and to send them this letter.*

*Please understand that I do not wish to cause this family undue anxiety in this matter. It is the child's well-being I have considered first and as I previously stated, my own peace of mind.*

*If the family decides to cooperate with my request for more information exchange, they may choose to go through a third party to maintain their privacy.*

*In any event I will appreciate and look forward to a response from you, the parents, or another third party in the near future, but no later than April 1, 1982; this should give the parents time to do some research (enclosed is a bibliography) if they choose to, so that they can understand more fully why I am so earnest in this situation.*

*Please accept my appreciation for your cooperation in this matter.*

*Sincerely,*

*Judy Bock Camera*

*P.S. Enclosed is a picture of myself you may also forward.*

I did not receive a response of any kind to this letter. But I persisted in other directions.

One was a letter that I sent to Vital Records in Oklahoma to be placed with her amended/original birth certificate.

*June 7, 1982*

*To Whom It May Concern,*

*I would like it known that if contact with me is wanted by the adoptive family or by the daughter, I surrendered for adoption after her birth April 7, 1969 I do give consent for contact.*

*I release any party from the restrictions of protecting my privacy so that contact may be made.*

*I should be able to be reached through my sister, Berniece Bock xxxxx (her address) or my lifetime friend,*

*Diane xxxxx (her address)*

*I would be most happy to meet her and/or her family as I have wondered how she fared and would like her to know more about me and her genetic heritage.*

*Sincerely,*

*Judith E. Bock R.N.*

*Birthdate 4-8-47*

*s.s. # xxx-xx-xxxx*

As I type this letter from the notebook I kept of documents related to Rose, I smile at the addition of R.N. after my signature. Was my intent to impress the government workers in the records office of my role in society as an upstanding citizen? It could be that it was an inadvertent mistake in that I automatically signed my name to lots of medical records throughout the day in my work life as a nurse.

As with so many communications during my search, I did not receive any acknowledgement of its being received or acted upon.

## Letter to my Obstetrician

*May 19, 1981 (Rose Diane was 12 at this time) Dear Dr. Maddox,*

*On April 7, 1969 you assisted in my delivery of a child at St. John's who I subsequently surrendered to adoption to a couple you knew.*

*I want to assure you that I have no desire to intrude on this family's privacy or to make any claim on this child. What I would like however is to make available to this family my name, address, and telephone number to be used at their discretion, if and when they feel the need for further information from me.*

*In the past year, I have done some reading and studying concerning the needs and problems facing adopted children and their families. I have been very interested to learn that recent studies indicate that children seek more information about their pre-adoption history than their adoptive parents can provide. Also adoptive parents themselves, in increasing numbers, are anxious to learn more about the people who conceived and bore the child they parent, in order to answer their children's questions, and have a better understanding of the child and the interplay of the environment they have provided with the heredity he has brought with him. The result of all this is a better mental and emotional health outlook for the child as well as his family.*

*It is in view of the above belief for the need for more information needed for the welfare of the child and the adoptive family that I release you of your obligation to protect my privacy and identity to this child's family.*

*I believe they will welcome this contact from you, and will not consider it an intrusion into their privacy. Further, it will give me considerable peace of mind to know that I am doing whatever I can to ensure that my releasing my child for adoption has not and will not put barriers in her path toward self-knowledge and self-respect.*

*Please give my request your serious consideration. I am enclosing a convenient checklist and SASE so that I can know what your response is.*

*Sincerely,*

*Judy Bock Camera*

*(my address in Wisconsin)*

*P.S. If you do not desire to participate in this request would you be willing to refer it to another third party such as a minister or social agency or lawyer?*

I did not receive any response from Dr. Maddox's office. I was left wondering if the information was provided to Rose Diane's family as I requested. It would have been a kindness for the doctor or a staff member in his clinic to take less than a minute to use the checklist I provided with the enclosed self-addressed stamped envelope. Maybe it got lost in the busy shuffle of office activity. It's interesting though, that during our meeting in 2018, Rose told me that her parents had at one point in her life asked her if she wanted more information about her birth family. "I don't need that," she told me she had responded. Maybe that was when she was 12 years old after they had received my offer from the doctor's office.

*June 25, 1982*

*State of Oklahoma*

*Dept. of Human Services Adoption Unit*

*P.O. Box 25352*

*Oklahoma City, OK 73125*

*Dear Human Services,*

*I have learned through Concerned United birth parents that you maintain a registry that could potentially facilitate the reunion of birth parents and their children.*

*I would like to apply to this registry. I surrendered a baby girl who was born April 7, 1969 at St. John's Hospital in Tulsa, Oklahoma delivered by Dr. James T. Maddox. She weighed 5# 15oz I was told. I was then Judith E. Bock and can be contacted through my sister:*

*Berniece Bock xxxxx (her address and phone)*

*I release you of any obligation to maintain my privacy.*

*Sincerely, Judy Bock*

*P.S. Please send a form if the above is inadequate.*

In response, I received a very official letter on the State of Oklahoma letterhead.

*August 30, 1982*

*Judith E. Bock*

*510 Ludington Avenue*

*Madison, WI 53704*

*Dear Ms. Bock:*

*We are in receipt of your recent letter in which you state that you would like to list your request to find your adopted child should your child make inquiries wanting to find you. You asked that your letter be listed on our registry. You gave your daughter's birthdate as 4-7-69.*

*This Department did not have custody of your child but we do have some information regarding the adoption. We have not heard from your daughter but, of course, she is not yet of age. Please be assured that we will list your request on our registry looking to the time when your daughter may make inquiries to locate you. Thank you for writing.*

*Very truly yours,*

*L. E. Rader,*

*Director of Human Services*

As I reread this letter many years later, I am struck by L.E. Rader's respectful tone and acknowledgement of my request. I think it was the first response I ever received after I made a request to some official or other during my search. Apparently, I sent at least two more letters to the Oklahoma Department of Human Services.

Another letter from the director is in my files, and again it was respectful, as I would expect a state official to be, but still I appreciate the response. It did not give me much information except that the department had made some sort of court report. As for the possibility that records may have been destroyed after five years, the thought comes to mind about the frequent response officials gave to adoption triad inquiries. That response was that records were destroyed by fire.

I am sure that in my inquiries I had not requested identifying information but rather non-identifying information that was often provided to birth parents around the time of adoption about the prospective adoptive family by many social service agencies and even private attorneys. Before surrendering my parental rights, I had never asked the attorney who represented the adoptive family for any such information. Many search advisors suggested asking for this non-identifying information when making inquiries in later years.

Here is a follow-up letter.

*October 13, 1982*

*Ms. Judith E. Bock*

*5156 Anton Drive #211*

*Madison, WI 53719*

*Dear Ms. Bock:*

*Please refer to the previous letter of August 30, 1982 and your subsequent correspondence and your recent correspondence of October 2, 1982. It will not be possible to give you detailed information about the adoptive family who adopted your child. This Department has some information on the adoptive family for the reason that the Department had to prepare a court report. There may or may not be any detailed information available for the reason that many of these cases are destroyed after five years.*

*Please be assured that your inquiry is listed on the registry just in case your daughter, when she becomes an adult, comes forward to this Department asking for information about her biological family.*

*Thank you for writing. (I think she/he probably would have liked to have written, "and please don't write again, we've told you all we can.")*

*Very truly yours,*

*L. E. Rader*

*Director of Human Services*

I again wrote to an Oklahoma official who I thought had access to my daughter's adoption file. This poor person must have started pulling his or her hair out when she got this letter, detailed as it is and apparently ignoring previous responses that little was available from their office.

*April 7, 1983*

*Director of Human Services*

*L.E. Rader and Attention Mrs. Jane Conner (I don't know why I added Conner's name)*

*Division of Child Welfare*

*P. O. Box 25352*

*Sequoyah Memorial Office Building*

*Oklahoma City, Oklahoma 73125*

*Dear L.E. Rader:*

*Thank you for your letter of October 13, 1982 in which you convey your reluctance to give me detailed information about the adoptive family of my child. It is my understanding of Oklahoma laws governing such situations that you are not required by law to withhold <u>non-identifying</u> information. I am specifically referring to Oklahoma Laws Governing Opening Records:*

*Children, Section 60.17 which prohibits access and inspection of court adoption records. If your understanding differs from mine, please be more specific as to which state law governs your actions.*

*If in reviewing your policy in regard to providing non-identifying information, you find you can answer some of my questions, I would be most grateful.*

*Questions I would like answered are the following:*

> *1.    Will all correspondence and information sent to your department by the birthfamily be placed in the record, and will it be given to the adoptee when requested?*

2.     Have any records of my case that were at one time held in your department's possession been destroyed? At what location or agency are copies presently on file?

3.     Will you notify me if my daughter in the future comes forward to request information about her birth family?

4.     Will you supply the following personal history of the adoptive family?

Parents Ages? Medical problem in family?

Where Born? Deaths in family? Causes?

Nationality? Diseases?

Parental Background? Education? Siblings on both sides? Religion?

Length of marriage? Physical descriptions?

Divorces?     Own their own home?

Other children in home? Professions? Occupations?

5.     Physical description of the child when last seen?

6.     What was the date the adoption was finalized?

7.     Was there any further action taken by courts regarding this child:

8.     What is the child's first name now?

9.     What foster homes, if any, was the child in?

10.    Reasons the adopters gave for adopting a child?

*11. How long a time passed between surrender and placement?*

*12. Has any contact been made with your department by the adoptee or the adoptive parents since the adoption was final? When? Reason?*

*13. Was the child returned to the hospital or doctor for any reason prior to the finalization of the adoption? When? Reason?*

*14. Were the adoptive parents advised to tell the child she was adopted?*

*Furthermore, in order that the files on this adoption are complete and correct, I request that you examine the records to see if the birth father was identified. I don't remember if I gave his name to the lawyer or the hospital. I have recently communicated with the birth father. We would like the records updated with the following information:*

*birth father's name: Josh xxxxx xxxxxx*

*Date of birth: x-xx-xx Place of birth: xxxxxx, xx*

*Present address: xxxx xxxxxx xxxxx, Springfield, MO Son's name: xxxxxxx xxxxxx xxxx of Ozark, MO Mother's name: xxxxxx xxxx xxxxxx*

*Father's name: xxxx xxxxxx xxxxxx*

*Thank you in advance for your prompt consideration and reply.*

*Sincerely,*

*Judith E. Bock*

*5156 Anton Drive #211*

*Madison, WI 53719*

*Cc Attorney Pamela Lunder and Josh xxxxx*

I apparently received no response to the letter of April 7, 1983, and sent a follow up.

*June 8, 1983*

*Director of Human Services*

*L.E. Rader and Attention Mrs. Jane Conner, Department of Human Services*

*Division of Child Welfare*

*P.O. Box 25352*

*Sequoyah Memorial Office building Oklahoma City, Oklahoma 73125*

*Dear L.E. Rader:*

*It has been over 60 days since my letter to you of April 7. Would you please inform me of the status of my request? I can understand the delay due to the nature of my letter but would like some sort of response in the near future.*

*Sincerely, Judith E. Bock*

*5156 Anton Dr. #211*

*Madison, WI 53119*

I can only assume that L.E. Rader had had enough of my continuing requests for information and the scope of it when she/he had thought it was clear that no such information was available or possible to give me. So Rader passed it on to a higher up. The following letter came July 6, 1983.

State of Oklahoma (letterhead)

*Oklahoma Commission for Human Services Department of Human Services*

*Ms. Judith E. Bock*

*5156 Anton Drive #211*

*Madison, Wisconsin 53719*

*Dear Ms. Bock:*

*We are in receipt of your letter of April 7, 1983. We have answered your request in the past on October 13, 1982 and August 30, 1982. Please note that this Department did not have custody of your child and did not arrange the adoption. The information available is very brief and the questions in your letter involve more information than this agency has.*

*Sometimes persons write in to this Department's Registry because the adoptee was adopted in Oklahoma though not placed by this Department. If we receive such an inquiry from your child we will contact you.*

*We would like to suggest that you contact the lawyer who arranged the adoption for you. He may have the information that you are seeking.*

*If you have any questions please feel free to contact Mrs. Jane xxxxx in our Adoption Section, at telephone number (405) 521-4373.*

*Sincerely, (signature of) Martha East for James Bonen, supervisor*

*Children's Services Unit*

I must say that I am grateful for the patience and courtesy in the correspondence I received from the Oklahoma Department of Human Services. Why I persisted in making inquiries to them must have been because I thought they were withholding information they had. The advice given to contact the lawyer who handled the adoption was good, and I tried to follow up on that as indicated by copies of letters to attorneys.

Thinking that I might have better success going directly to some of the offices that had information about me and the adoption seemed to be a good idea at the time. Sometimes face to face contact yields better results than phone calls or letters.

Following some of the tips of search organizations, I planned a trip to Tulsa for August of 1983. My notes in preparation for the trip indicate I planned to make numerous inquiries of the OB doctor, the attorney, the district attorney and probate court. I am amazed by the persistence and zeal I possessed at that time in my life.

Under doctor, I wrote the following:

*Waiver of confidentiality on file?*

1. *Name of Dr/hospital changed on birth certificate — consent should be on file?*
2. *Paternity documented*
3. *Info on family — religion, Tula residents then, now?*

4.  *How soon after birth did she go to an adoptive home?*

5.  *My name on any documents given to parents?*

I believe I hoped to get these questions answered during a visit to the OB doctor's office.

For the attorney, I have the following questions in my file that I had hoped I could get answered during my trip to Tulsa.

> 1. *Waiver of confidentiality on file?*
>
> 2. *Info on family — religion, Tulsa residents then, now?*
>
> 3. *Letter to adoptive parents from me to last known address. How will I know it was received?*
>
> 4. *How soon after birth did she go to adoptive home?*
>
> 5. *Name of lawyer who handled case — still alive?*
>
> 6. *Can I leave letter with court in case she petitions them?*

The lawyer who visited with me numerous times and filled out paperwork on the adoptive parent's behalf was in Tulsa's Petroleum Building. I had no luck getting an appointment with him because he was no longer in practice, apparently retired or deceased. I eventually learned who took over his files, and I visited her office during that trip. It was a memorable visit, not because of the information I received about my daughter's placement or answers to my prepared questions, but an ironic and sad conversation I had with the receptionist there.

As I recall, she was a pretty, young slender woman who said she was the attorney's daughter. She became tearful when I told her I was seeking information related to a child I had placed for adoption and further conversation. "I had a baby that I put up for adoption two years ago," she told me. "My mother arranged for the adoption." Her grief was still there with her and came to the surface quickly. She perhaps had better access to her child's adoptive journey than I did, I remember thinking.

She gave me the impression that she tried to find my file but couldn't. It was no doubt under the adoptive family's name, as they were the attorney's clients, not me. I only provided the child. She told me state court records were sealed and stored at the "Old Depot" and could only be opened through a petition of the court.

My attempt to get information from an attorney was unsuccessful. I wondered what effect my inquiry had on the still grieving birth mother working in that office.

Other notes I kept in my file were about going to the district attorney's office to see if paternity was documented, if my name was on the surrender, what my rights still are, and locating the attorney. I have a name and number in my notes, but I don't recall any results from that avenue.

"Call Probate court secretary — where are indexes kept?" is another note, followed by the apparent result "county court clerk — 584-0471 → no help."

Before the trip, I called and made an appointment at the obstetrician's office and learned that Dr. Maddox, who had delivered Rose, was no longer in the office and, in fact, had died since her birth. Knowing that records were usually kept for an undetermined period of time, I had made an appointment with one of the other physicians in the obstetric group. When I met with the doctor in the exam room, he came in with a thin file. Upon telling him why I came, he glanced through the chart quickly and said something to the effect that Dr. Maddox was not known for writing a lot of notes, and the ones that he did were in very bad handwriting. None of my questions got answered during this trip to Oklahoma.

## Correspondence with Search Organizations

In addition to public officials, I contacted people in the adoption triad community who were known to be helpful in searches. Following are letters of mine to searchers and some of their responses.

*November 28, 1982*

*Jan xxxx*

*Tulsa, Oklahoma*

*Dear Jan,*

*As per our conversation on the phone today I'm sending you the particulars regarding the child I gave birth to in Tulsa in hopes you can provide me with non-identifying information about her and also communicate to the parents that I am available to update information, medical or otherwise, that they might need to help their child in her development.*

*Birth date: April 7, 1969*

*Place: St. John's, Tulsa*

*Wt: 5 # 15 oz*

*Doctor: Maddox*

*Pediatrician: Miller*

*Adoption proceedings in Tulsa* (Unknown to me at the time of this letter, was that Rose's adoption took place in Lawrence, Kansas. All my entreaties to Oklahoma officials had been misdirected and wasted effort.)

*Thank you for taking the time to help me, the child, and indirectly her parents.*

*I realize I'll never be a parent to this child as I signed away my legal rights. I did not however sign away my human right to continue having concern for her welfare.*

*Sincerely,*

*Judy Bock (Judith Ellen)*

*Birth date: x-xx-xxxx*

*P.S. Enclosed is an SASE. Also feel free to contact me via phone and call collect 608-271-2073. Address: 5156 Anton Dr. #211 Madison, WI 53719*

*P.S. Please bill me for any expenses you may incur.*

I do not find a direct response from Jan in my files, but did receive a typed letter on Southwest Missouri Adult Adoptees Assoc. letterhead from Elizabeth xxxxx, who referred to Jan as a possible contact who might help in searching.

*June 1, 1983*

*Lidia xxxx*

*(Oklahoma address)*

*Dear Lidia,*

*It was good to meet you in* Columbus (This would have been at one of the national conferences of the American Adoption Conference, an organization I belonged to and respected.)

*I am happy to know there is activity in Oklahoma that is helpful to adoptees and birth parents who seek reunions.*

*You asked me to send you my personal statistics in the hope it will aid me in the eventual reunion with my daughter.*

*Name: Baby Girl Bock (I didn't know at the time that I could have given her a name.) Place of Birth: St. John's Hospital, Tulsa, Oklahoma*

*Date and Time: April 7, 1968 at 8:29 p.m.*

*Birth wt: 5# 15 oz.*

*Attending OB physician: Dr. J. T. Maddox Pediatrician: Dr. Miller*

*Private Adoption through Tulsa County Court, present attorney Xxx Xxxxxxxx of Tulsa. (Xxx was not the attorney I dealt with, but she was referred to me by Judge Wiseman of Tulsa District Court. My searching with this misinformation that the adoption took place in Tulsa did not help.)*

*I'd very much appreciate any help you can give me in my search. I hope to find that she was placed in a happy, stable home, but the truth, whatever it is, is better than wondering forever.*

*I am very interested in any legislative activity in Oklahoma and would appreciate your contacting me by letter (SASE) enclosed or collect call. (608) 271-2973*

*I'll enclose a copy of my waiver of confidentiality I left with the doctor (Maddox) and attorney in Tulsa last year.*

*Thanks again for your help. God bless you and your work.*

*Sincerely,*

*Judy Bock*


*June 29, 1983*

*Judy Bock*

*(Wisconsin Address)*

*Dear Judy:*

*I guess you thought you would never hear from me. I had a fire and what mail was not destroyed was misplaced. I am just now going to get around to answering my older mail.*

*Normally I would have answered within days ... and will try to do better next time. I am enclosing anything I mail in a package to anyone who inquires of me for information.*

*First, let me tell you that I grew up in .......xxxx Missouri ... (she gave me information about her family, her husband's family and other personal information ...) We moved to Springfield in 1972 and have been here since. I worked at St. John's Hospital from Oct. '72-Dec. '75. Strange how lives cross???* (Apparently, in previous contact with her, I had told her I grew up in a town close to where she did and had gone to nursing school at St. John's Hospital prior to her working there. Whether this was a conversation I had with her at an adoption conference or through the mail I don't know.)

*We do ask for a $10 donation to help keep the mail going out and the phones ringing. I hope some of this is helpful.*

*Some suggested contacts:*

*Lidia*

*(her address)*

*Jan xxxx*

*(Her address and phone)*

*Jean xxxxxxxx*

*(Her address and phone)*

*Let me know if I can do anything else to help you. If you do decide to make a trip to Springfield, Mo., in the future, let me know. Hoping to hear from you again soon.*

*Sincerely, Elizabeth A. xxxxx*

At the bottom of the page of Elizabeth's letter:

*"A small candle burning in a universe of darkness."*

*Information and support for Adoptees and Birth Parents and anyone "disconnected" from roots. Meetings 2nd Saturday each month.*

*Volunteers available for panel discussions and speaking engagements.*


I have no follow up information in my file regarding Elizabeth's letter. I reached out in many directions hoping to find some help with my search.

I learned much later that my child's adoption was not finalized in Oklahoma as I had thought, but rather in Kansas, close to where her adoptive parents lived at that time. I deduced that they had both grown up in Oklahoma and knew people in the Tulsa area who must have referred them to Dr. Maddox for a source of a baby to adopt. My friend, Diane, had told me that Dr. Maddox had a reputation of facilitating adoptions for wealthy and respected families.

I did not find it in my files, but I recall getting a letter from an Oklahoma triad searcher who informed me that she could not be of assistance because her policy was to only help searchers in which the adoptee was 18.

Another letter, written on a unique letterhead of a triad searcher, is typical of the kindness of persons in the adoption community.

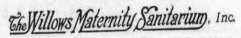

A SECLUSION MATERNITY
SANITARIUM OPERATED EXCLUSIVELY
FOR THE CARE AND PROTECTION OF
THE BETTER CLASS OF UNMARRIED
YOUNG WOMEN
ADDRESS ALL COMMUNICATIONS TO
THE WILLOWS
MRS. DON D. HAWORTH, SUPT.
TELEPHONE WESTPORT 1-2104
MRS. MAUDENE LOWE, ASST. SUPT.
MRS. NELLE T. McEWEN, SEC'Y.

MEMBER
MISSOURI HOSPITAL ASSOCIATION
MID-WEST HOSPITAL ASSOCIATION
AMERICAN HOSPITAL ASSOCIATION

REFERENCE:
THE JACKSON COUNTY MEDICAL SOCIETY

OPEN TO ANY REPUTABLE PHYSICIAN
ESTABLISHED 1905

The Willows Maternity Sanitarium, Inc.

2929 MAIN STREET
KANSAS CITY 8, MISSOURI

The Willows Maternity Sanitarium
Kansas City, Missouri
(Willows in Old Days)

"Superior Babies for Adoption
at the Nursery of the Willows,
2929 Main Street, Kansas City,
Missouri."

*Letterhead of one of the homes for unwed mothers in Kansas City, Missouri, that becomes the later letterhead of an adoption search and reunion adoptee who called herself a "Willows Graduate."*

*Dear Judy,*

*Thank you for your letter, coming from Wis, gee my mother (natural) lived in Whitewater Wis.*

*Now, I do only Willows, from K.C. Mo. but will give you a few addresses of people we know that may be able to help you.*

266

*#1 Dean xxxxx (with an Oklahoma City, Oklahoma address and phone number) #2 Lidia xxxxx (with an Oklahoma City, Oklahoma address and phone number)*

*You will have to tell them more info, where child was born etc. All info is in Okla City about Okla adoptions.*

*I have no fees etc., just do it from love for others, but as I said I do only Willows. Good luck!*

*Love Jeanne       — over—*

*I do believe if you're able to call you will do better, people are so pressed for time.*

*June xxxx also does lots of Okla work; her address is (and gave a Tulsa address and phone)*

*If your child was born in Tulsa, she has great leads; she hasn't been well so if you think she is near your birth area call her also.*


The following is a detailed letter I wrote to a searcher who agreed to help me:

*July 17, 1984*

*Dear xxxxx,*

*It was encouraging to talk to you yesterday on the phone. I've gathered together copies of correspondence I have on hand with people I've contacted in my search for Baby Girl Bock.*

*In addition, I have contacted the following with request for search help with no success:*

*1)      Lidia xx xxxx (her address and phone number)*

*She is friendly to me but will not search until my daughter is 18 and then seems skeptical of success.*

*2) Elizabeth xxxxx (her address)*

*She is involved with a triad group in Springfield, MO, was co-operative, but we just never got into my search too much.*

*3) Xxxx Xxxxxx, Attorney (her address)*

*She was referred to me by Jane Wiseman, Judge of the District court in Tulsa where I signed surrender papers.*

*I wrote and personally spoke with Xxxx Xxxxxx Xxxx and her daughter who works in her office, who denied being able to locate any records on Baby Bock's adoption.*

*The attorney who I dealt with for the adoption was xxxx xxxxx of Tulsa who is no longer in practice and may be dead by now.*

*I have a friend in Tulsa who has a friend, a lawyer who is a friend of Judge Wiseman.*

*The lawyer friend was asked by my friend to ask Judge Wiseman to forward a letter from me to the adoptive parents. She refused. This was since Aug. of '83.*

*4) Dr. Deardorff (Office address and phone)*

*I had an appointment with Dr. Deardorff in Aug. of 83 in his office to seek information about Baby Bock and her adoptive family. He had my records, however he said there was little information he could give me as none was put in my record. Dr. Deardorff was in partnership with J.T. Maddox, my obstetrician who together with Mr. xxxx, arranged an independent adoption. Dr. Maddox died a couple of years ago of cancer. I note that Dr. Miller is listed as the baby's pediatrician, but I have never contacted that office.*

*It might be useful to know of my other names having been married and divorced twice since 1969. In January of 1970 I married xxxxxxx x xxxx and took his name. We were divorced in December of 1974 and I returned to my maiden name of Bock. In May of 1977 I married x.x. xxxxx and took the name of Judith Bock xxxxx. Our divorce hearing was in July of 1982 at which time I returned to my maiden name and still do at this writing.*

*I am a member of CUB and formerly a CUB rep. (CUB stands for Concerned United Birth Parents) I am a lifetime member of the American Adoption Conference. I am a member of the local triad group here in Wisconsin, Adoption Information and Direction.*

*I can generally be contacted at any time since I am not presently working outside my home. I do travel frequently with my husband, xxxx xxxxxxxxx. My home phone number is (608) 836-xxxx.*

*Again, congratulations to you on the success of your search and best of luck to you in your relationship with your daughter.*

*Sincerely,*

*Judith E. Bock 6905 North Ave.*

*Middleton, WI 53562*

*P.S. I almost forgot to thank you for your efforts in my search. I will keep you informed of any new developments.*

## Sources for More Information

The American Adoption Congress, 1030 15th St. NW, Suite B-103, Washington, DC 20005

https://www.americanadoptioncongress.org/

Concerned United Birthparents, P.O. Box 703486 Dallas, TX 75370 https://concernedunitedbirthparents.org/

International Soundex Reunion Registry, P.O. Box 371179, Las Vegas, NV 89137 http://www.isrr.org/index.htm


## Recommended Reading/Watching

The following will not be a complete list but will include sources I found valuable.

Lost and Found by Betty Jean Lifton, Ph.D.

The Adoption Triangle by Arthur D. Sorosky, M.D, Annette Baran, M.S.W., Reuben Pannor, M.S.W.

Dear Birth Parent by Kathleen Silber and Phylis Speedlin

How it Feels to be Adopted by Jill Krementz

The Girls Who Went Away by Ann Fessler

To Seek and to Find by Liz Gardner

The Story of Molly and Me by Fran Levin

Georgia Tann: Memphis Baby Adoption Scandal, a documentary on YouTube by Jerry Skinner at:

https://www.youtube.com/watch?v=B2qhVQR5u08

Stolen Babies 1993 movie starring Mary Tyler Moore as Georgia Tann.


## Baylor University Study on Birth Mother Satisfaction with Decision

I tried to find research related to birth parent experience after relinquishment. It was hard to find. I think that many birth parents keep pretty quiet about this part of their lives, not necessarily because of shame, but it is a sensitive subject not shared with anyone but trusted family, friends, or health care providers.

I did run across a study done at Baylor University, ironically the college my daughter attended, about an online survey of 223 birth mothers to determine their satisfaction with the adoption decision. It was published in Science News in 2018. The Science News article leads with the following statement, "There is consensus among adoption researchers that for many birth mothers, the experience of placing their children for adoption brings feelings of grief, loss, shame, guilt, remorse and isolation."

What Baylor's study sought to learn was how the level of satisfaction changed over time.

The report outlines five findings with some elaborations that I summarize from the original report.

Satisfaction about the decision to place a child for adoption by birth mothers in the study changed over time to less satisfaction later in life for some birth mothers. More dissatisfaction with the decision occurred after achieving higher education and income later in life. The researchers suggested this may have occurred with the realization by the birth mother that they would have actually been capable of raising the child.

Another of these researchers' findings made perfect sense to me. This was the finding that birth mothers with current contact with their child were more likely to have satisfaction with the decision than others who did not.

A final conclusion of the study was that birth mothers in the study who worked full time had more satisfaction. My interpretation of this final result is that perhaps they had less time on their hands to think about it and come to the conclusion of regret.

But this was a small study of only 200 plus birth mother subjects, hardly a definitive one.

Study authors readily admit to the need for further study of the subject of birth mother satisfaction.

For the complete article, go to: "Are Birth Mothers Satisfied with decisions to place children for adoption?" at:

-https://www.sciencedaily.com/releases/2018/06/180608131605. htm

# Poems by Judith Bock

## *The Pierced Heart*

*Fireworks, wreaths, and candles*

*evoke uncontrolled surges from hollow places.*

*Pain-wrenching, alarming, ferocious grasps*

*take the unsuspecting.*

*Clutched in remembered loss, the careening cor falters*

*as arrows plunge deeply.*

*Leaving salty blood*

*tasting on her lips, falling unattended — noted still.*

*To wrestle free from pursuing arrows — a struggle, a flight,*

*a wild-eyed escape.*

*Meandering dreams unfulfilled in time and imaginings with*
*wakening to new Cinderella tales.*

*Always another turn, plan the voyage this time*

*and watch eagles soar.*

*Join in the flight, no backward glancing*

*She starts again alone, herself beside as friend.*

I wrote "The Pierced Heart" around 1995 after a marriage breakup. It reflected my feelings of loneliness and disillusionment of "happiness ever after." It certainly voices deep emerging emotions of sadness and pain that "grasps" me, "the unsuspecting." In trying to relate this to my loss of Rose, the line "Clutched in remembered loss" reflects my disappointment at yet another loss of a relationship.

# The Place not Set

*She should be here, But she's not.*

*Smiles, hugs, laughter, food.*
*A bar of drinks, leftover wedding cake.*

*Pictures, smiles, flash and snap.*
*Shutter-speed fast — like a signature — then gone.*

*The deep chest pain comes to the throat, Spills down my cheeks*
*— over and over, Unending, then stops.*

*Until the next family event.*

I wrote "The Place not Set" in August of 1996 after a nephew's wedding. I wrote it to express my sorrow after this large, happy family event and to show my disappointment at not having Rose in my life.

There were many camera flashes at the wedding that I compare to the lightning-fast speed of a signature ending my parentage to Rose.

275

*Author, center front, regrets not having her daughter join in on this 1995 family canoe trip and other family events.*

# Love-15, Her Serve

*It was a day of stormy rain as I traveled to a burger place.*

*Would I find what I was looking for when I met her face to face?*


*A decision made when I was young left me sad with regret when once awake.*

*I had no counsel, was not informed. I often wondered, "Was it a mistake?"*


*But then I came to a place agreed, found welcome arms and smiles.*

*For the first time ever I held my lovely child — so worth the traverse of thunderous miles.*


*I gathered gifts I gave to her. "They hold significance," I said.*

*A golden chain of infinite love, a floral plate, a bag of corn, an intricate circle of thread.*


*"They look alike," so many say when their images they behold.*

*A combination of nature and nurture — I ponder these words experts foretold.*

*I admire the courage she must have had to defy those who said no to our meeting.*

*A chance to share if only briefly*

*an hour and 15 minutes — so fleeting!*


*But now I feel great joy and peace as I settle back to my life once more.*

*I have my memories, our photos are framed. Now the ball is in her court — just as before.*


Love-15, Her Serve is a poem I wrote to my daughter after our meeting for the first time.

# Bill of Rights for Birth Parents Before Relinquishment

*Birth parents have the right to see and hold their newborn.*

*Birth parents have the right to full knowledge of their baby's health until adoption.*

*Birth parents have the right to name their child.*

*Birth parents have the right to review social service or other assessments of potential adoptive parents.*

*Birth parents have a right to meet with and interview potential adoptive parents.*

*Birth parents have the right to choose the adoptive parents for their child.*

*Birth parents have a right to hire a lawyer to represent them prior to, during and after signing relinquishment papers.*

*Birth parents have a right to know if, and how long they have, to change their minds about relinquishment after signing consent papers.*

*Birth parents have a right to be free of all sedating or other mind altering drugs prior to signing relinquishment papers.*

*Birth parents have the right to care for their infant after birth until relinquishment is finalized.*

*Birth parents have a right to require an open adoption for their child in which continued exchange of information and in-person visits are allowed.*

*Birth parents have all the rights any parent has regarding their child until relinquishment papers are signed.*

Note: These rights are of my own authorship; nonetheless, I believe them to be valid. Relinquishment and adoption laws in the United States vary from state to state. Open adoption contracts are not enforceable in many states.

Made in the USA
Monee, IL
22 May 2024

58774410R00164